A Five-Step Formula to Land Your Dream Job

ADAM REITER

Library of Congress Cataloging-in-Publication Data

Reiter, Adam, 1972-
    You can get a job in fashion :
        a five step formula to land your dream job/Adam Reiter.
    Includes bibliographically references and appendices
    ISBN 978-0-615-26119-5 (pbk.)
    1. Clothing trade-Vocational guidance.
    2. Fashion-Vocational guidance. I. Title.

Library of Congress Control Number: 2008910154

The Job Tool © 2008
ISBN 978-0-615-26119-5

CONTENTS:

INTRODUCTION

You love fashion; you feel it in your bones. You may not know exactly what kind of job you will pursue, but you know you will work in fashion. Or, some of you may just fall into it like I did. Even though I didn't go to school for fashion and even though I am far from a style icon, I think I was destined to work in fashion. I was raised by the original super-shopper, my mom. I spent more time in Saks Fifth Avenue than on a soccer field. I knew more about fabrics than football. I can understand now why it seemed awkward that I spent more time shopping with momma than surfing with my buddies. Well, now I am spending time with you talking about fashion jobs and that's pretty cool. So all my time in boutiques as a kid is paying off.

This book is for the fashionistas, the fashionistos—those with the passion for fashion and those with an eye for everything fabulous! There is no magic, luck or nepotism necessary to get a great job in fashion. You don't need to be rich, Olsen Twin skinny or have an uncle who owns the haute fashion company. What you need to do is take everything you have heard, known or seen in relation to your job search and throw it out the window. You need a different type of guide for this journey. Lucky for you, I am just the right kind of crazy to help you beat a new path toward a wonderful and rewarding career in fashion.

This Book Is For…

Are you a college student, high school student, fashion veteran or just curious about the fashion business? I wrote this book for students, but the methods apply to all seekers. At the end of the day, finding an internship requires the same formula as finding that senior executive job. Sure, the resume and experiences are different, but the techniques aren't.

I saved my intro for last. I wanted to make sure that I provided a realistic view of the marketplace, what it takes to be successful and, most importantly, a real-world perspective. I didn't want to spoon feed you with loads of candy-coated nothingness. There are plenty of those books out there. I wanted to give you insight into the true fashion job market, real jobs and a real formula for success. And, this is my way of warming you up for my casual way of speaking and sometimes, unorthodox advice. But keep in mind, most of the successful people we all know are mavericks.

The Approach

My approach to job searching is formulaic. While this approach is different than what I have seen from other career guides, it does employ a step-by-step method. I like steps, little tiny baby steps. It makes us feel good to accomplish a small goal. Immediately having the next small step to accomplish makes the journey feel attainable and fosters momentum towards the ultimate goal. Sounds good so far, right?

THE FIVE STEPS

This book will take you through the five steps of your job search.

The First Step–Identification:
This is an easy place to start. Many of you may be set on a specific career goal. Read through this step anyway, you may learn about some cool related jobs or learn something new about the job(s) you are going for.

The Second Step–Building A Winning Resume:
This step will steer you through the delicate art of resume creation. I hated writing resumes until I learned how to write them effectively. Putting off writing my resume was a skill I developed easily. However, writing a winning resume was a skill I learned just as easily once I knew the secrets. Everybody loves a good secret and I have loads of them…they will make you and your wallet very happy.

The Third Step–Research and Stuff:
This is a fun exercise. Basically, all I ask you to do is list your favorite fashion companies and learn how to research like a pro. These are the companies that you may work for one day and I give you all the tools, clues and tricks for your search. Do you like being a detective? You will become your own job search sleuth in no time.

The Fourth Step–Creative Submission Strategy:
This strategic step is the way in which you get, rather, capture the attention of companies you want to work for. This is how you make companies want you. This is the most significant success factor in counter intuitive job searching and it is fashion-job-search gold. Forget sending your resume to a big black hole, the techniques in this step will get you results.

The Fifth Step–The Interview:
And finally, the cherry on your fashion-job-search sundae. Interviews aren't tough, it's just like dating. I'll show you the techniques to make your interviews the best ever! And as a bonus, this technique also works in dating, who knew?!

That's it! The Five Steps of my program are a simple formula for success that has worked for thousands of fashion trend-setters just like you. Are you ready? You CAN Get A Job In Fashion!

step one:
IDENTIFICATION

So, you've got all of that passion for fashion, but how do you translate that desire into a career? Many of you will say that "Buying" is your passion. Many of you will say that "Design" is your passion. Some of you might not know the different kinds of gigs available in fashion, but you love love love the industry and you're determined to make it your career. Excellent! Well, this section will be a big help to you because it will discuss popular jobs and lesser known, but equally awesome jobs. These goodies will include salary ranges, expected career path and ease of entry. Look, some gigs are just easier to get than others because they are deemed less sexy or are just less known. But trust me, I will not steer you towards yucky jobs, but rather, give you my honest take on what these fashion jobs are and maybe, more importantly, what they are not. Dispelling the myths… I am your guru of fashion career truth. At least for this section, I am.

The Popular Gigs:

There are many popular gigs in fashion. These are the jobs that everybody wants, students and veterans alike. Some of the positions I get asked about most often are design, buying, styling, merchandising, public relations and marketing jobs. I will cover all of these. By the time I am done, you will be an expert on these popular fashion jobs, I promise.

A Disclaimer

But before I go on, I need to list a disclaimer. This book will not cover starting a business. It will not address how to open a boutique or start a clothing line.

At the back of this book, I have included a list of jobs in fashion with a brief definition, salary info and more. Check it out.

back-of-the-book

Why? That is an entirely different book and while I applaud anyone with the intestinal fortitude to start a new business, I want you to get some experience under your belt and make contacts in the industry before you ask, Mom, Vegas, Visa, Uncle Sam and everyone else for the cash to start something "awesome."

Fashion Jobs:

Designer

Alright, so, you want to be a DESIGNER. You want to rip up the runways, lunch with Stella McCartney and Lagerfeld, splash onto the cover of Vogue and be a star! Awesome. Me, too! Who doesn't want that?! What's not cool about being a designer? Creating haute frocks that you know in your very core that Madge, Gwen and Paris would Rock…how cool would that be? Okay, there are two kinds of designers in this world, the ones that design for love and the ones that design for money. The money part is relative, of course. Some designers who design the avant garde do make money, but even they rarely make the big bucks.

"Designing For Dollars"

I spoke at a college and a student who hated this statement. She cited Ralph Lauren as a designer that designs for love **and** makes huge money. Yes, an awesome example of an American success story–I am an avid consumer of Mr. Lauren's products. This multi-billion dollar empire is built on a lifestyle, a fashion brand that millions around the world connect with. Ralph figured out what many successful fashion designers have done to make big money. You design product for the masses if you want to dine with the classes. This is an old cliché, but a true one. If Ralph didn't sell his product through licenses and to the Macy's of the world–the retail middle–he wouldn't have a billion dollar company. While he develops a pedigree for his brand through his luxury Ralph Lauren Purple Label and RRL Lines, we buy the Polo, Polo Jeans and Lauren labels that float his giant company. So yes, he does do both. He still makes great "for the love" product, but also makes licensing deals and creates mass-market product "for the money." You can design anything you want, work for any brand, but you need to figure out what you want from this industry. At some point designers need to make a choice on how they will survive. It isn't all about glitz and glamour, dollars and sense also play a paramount role in fashion.

Is It Time To Bust A Design?

It is a crazy-exciting time to be a fashion designer. It used to be that American fashion broke quickly in NY and LA and then lagged as the fashion trend waves rolled slowly over the rest of the country. Not so much, anymore. Thanks to the fashion reality shows, the fashion magazines, e-zines and blogs, fashion is everywhere. Companies like MNG by Mango, Zara and H&M have landed in the US selling us fast-fashion–clothes that are both inexpensive and on-trend. This means that companies who sell five-years-ago fashion to the Mall of America are now racing to build their design teams to meet the overwhelming need for fashion-forward product. The gap between "for love" and "for money" is closing and that is amazing.

Top 5 Ways You Know You are a Designer:

5- When your best friend Jenny asks you if you like her new capris and you say, "That's so 1999."

4- You go up to mannequins in stores and give them a good feel to check the fabric and see how stuff was cut.

3- You can't pass a bead or fabric store without popping in.

2- You doodle silhouettes at dinner.

1- You know what a jacquard is.

Designer Skills That Pay The Bills

On one level it's all about taste, a certain sense of style or your ability to forecast trends. But, there is a very real technical side to being a great designer, as well. You have to, have to, **have to** be proficient with the design program, Adobe Illustrator. Being proficient in Adobe Photoshop is important, too. These industry standard programs are the NOW of how fashion design works. Being able to sketch on the computer is paramount and if you can continuously invest in your skills with these programs you will be far ahead of the rest of the pack. Another technical aspect of design is clothing construction. Washes, fabric weights, marking, grading, draping, patternmaking–understanding all of these technical aspects of garment construction are key in being a successful designer. Most designers laugh when I ask them if they are good sales people, but it is not enough just to be creative. You have to sell your product. *You have to sell your designs to your design team, sales teams, buyers and ultimately, to the consumer.* Your passion has to translate into products that people want to sell and buy. In reality, every great designer is also a great sales person. If the individual I just detailed sounds like you, you might just be the next big designer, or at least one that can pay for those Italian shoes.

If you haven't already, check out Adobe's Creative Suite of Software. You will need to know these products well if you want to be a designer. Log onto www.adobe.com

Cash and Path

How much you can earn depends largely on you, of course. The sky is the limit, literally. Top top design executives can easily make a seven figure salary. Now, that's a lot of Louis Vuitton! Most Assistant Designers start out at between $20,000-35,000 per year. An associate level designer can expect to make between $40,000-60,000 per year. Designers and Sr. Designers can make between $50,000-$140,000 per year. Design Directors can make between $100,000-300,000. The top line design managers, Vice Presidents or Sr. Vice Presidents of Design can make between $300,000 to over $1,000,000 per year!

The Assistant Designer

Let's face it, most entry-level jobs are "go-for" jobs. You have to go for coffee and go for copies and go for supplies. However, when you aren't just doing other people's errands, you're marinating. You get the time to absorb knowledge, learn how the design department works and communicates with the other departments in a design company. You get to learn the development process, first hand. You learn about the life cycle of a garment from inception to delivery. An intimate knowledge of theses processes are a critical foundation you will need as a designer.

Along side of your seemingly endless "go-for" duties, you will get to sketch and color–here's where those good Illustrator skills come in. You will create **tech packs**, communicate with vendors and will likely visit factories. There is a lot to learn in this entry-level job. And remember, how well you do at this level may determine how fast you move through the ranks.

Tech Pack-Defined:
A tech pack is a document or series of documents that call out all of the technical details necessary to produce a product correctly. This information is translated from the design department through the pre-production departments all the way to production.

The Associate Designer

Hey, if you work for a larger company at the associate level then you probably aren't at the bottom rung anymore. That means you may have someone working under you who can do your errands, your own "go-for." You have hit easy street, baby! Well, probably not, but the good news is that you will have more responsibility in actually creating designs and that's what this is all about, right! Ah, finally, you get to show your skills and translate the company's design vision into spot-on product. While, you probably won't have free reign at this level you will get a better feel for what the next level up will mean to your career. And, all of that knowledge you slurped up at the Assistant level will start paying off.

The Designer

You are finally there, a designer, the job you have planned and worked so hard for, awesome! But wait, what is all this management and budget stuff? I didn't sign up for this. Yes, you will have responsibilities outside of creating and developing designs. You will need to help manage your staff, negotiate with vendors and be fully aware of your departmental budgets. You will need to be more active with your pre-production and production teams. You may even have significant interaction with your sales teams and be involved in meetings with buyers. Hey, it's a big job, but the rewards of having a team supporting you *and* being able to execute great product makes the responsibility well worth it.

The Job of a Design Director

When I meet students, this is what they envision. Being the top dog, el jefe, da man...umm...da woman. When I met my wife, she was a lowly assistant designer for a popular action sports apparel company. When she spoke about design and fashion she always ended with, "When I'm a Design Director..." That was her measuring stick for her career success. The dream was that she could go back to her little town where she grew up outside of Minneapolis and tell all of her teachers, classmates and relatives that she made it. I believe the quote was, to all the nay sayers, "In your face!" Well, she got there with all of her hard work and moxie. The funny part is, since she has achieved her goal and been home numerous times, there hasn't been even one instance where she proclaimed her success. Like many of you will experience, her journey came with a gradual settling and a quiet growth of self-confidence. She had already answered to the only one who mattered–herself. No "in your face" moment necessary.

But, I digress. As a design director, you are probably the head of the design department and with this comes a lot of responsibility and a lot of reward. You will have to manage your budget for the department which may include: salaries, raises, trips, entertainment, fit models, sampling, prints, supplies and more. You will partner with the heads of the other departments to understand their needs and translate yours. You will be involved in recruiting and developing your staff.

You will plan inspiration trips and competitive shopping trips to see what your competition is doing and what product is trending at the cash registers. Your design responsibilities will vary from overall line concept to seasonal direction to trim and fabric development to color palettes. And, there is so much more. This is a big and rewarding job both financially and professionally.

Employee Development:

Employee Development is key to your success in any position. When you are interviewing for positions, speak to people that have worked or are currently working for companies that you are interested in. Find out which managers really take the time to develop/train their staff. When you bust your behind for an employer, you want to make sure that part of the deal includes the training you need to move to the next level. Your ability to sniff out which managers and companies do this will be a big key to your success.

The Vice President of Design

Let me start by saying not all design companies have a VP of Design. These positions are rather scarce. But, they still do exist at many large design houses and **vertical retailers.**

These people make bucks, big bucks. I remember sitting with a client, a large vertical retailer and they were talking about therapy bills. Because I'm nosey and always looking for a good therapist, I asked, "Got a good shrink?" They explained they were bringing on a new VP of Design and hoped they wouldn't have to pick up the tab for the psycho therapy like they had to with the last VP of Design. Huh? Yes, not only did they pay this guy a seven figure salary, but they also paid for his weekly check up. I guess when you are at the top of the food chain, it makes sense for a company to keep you sane. But, a million dollar salary isn't enough to pay for the therapist? Must be quite a doc.

When you reach the pinnacle of design management, you truly are just that, a manager. You are responsible for building and maintaining a team of professionals. You are responsible for maintaining budgets and margins. Of course, you also have a significant role in trend forecasting and setting the tone and concepts for your brand(s). It's a big job, but that's why these guys and girls get the BIG Bucks!

Retail Jobs

Buyer

I want you to imagine a job where you jet to international fashion shows, get taken out to the most expensive restaurants in town and shop all day…how rad does that sound? Most people who think they have amazing style–and who want to be buyers–imagine buying to be as described above. The description is kind of true and kind of not. Yes, you will go to fashion/trade shows maybe even some overseas. Yes, vendors will try to ply you with booze and beef (in that order). And, yes, you do get to buy stuff, a lot of stuff. But, it's not all glam.

Buyer Skills That Pay The Bills

Here's the dose of reality to add to your fantasy job. You have to be a bit of a math nerd because your buying parameters are set by historical data: what sold, what didn't, what trends, what doesn't. There are a lot of spreadsheets to be read as a buyer and you have a holy grail that hangs over your head and it's name is, **GMROI.**

Buying is a business job. Gross Margin Return on Inventory Investment or GMROI ("Jim-Roy") is the foundation for how buyers buy and retailers stay afloat.

Buying is an awesome job for someone with a business head and a yen for shopping (not all buying is fashion; there's electronics, books, software, etc.). Even if you're not a math wiz or don't have a huge business head, don't worry, this still maybe the gig for you.

Vertical Retailer-Defined:
A vertical retailer is a company that manufacturers the product they sell. For instance, *The Gap* is a vertical retailer because it sells its own branded product and not usually product from other brands.

GMROI-Defined:
GMROI is a comparative measure. It enables you to compare the performance of merchandise departments, vendors, stores, even customer groups!

I Am Not the End-All Be-All Judge of Talent (but, I think I am)

For years, I have had formulas in my head from my experiences as a recruiter as to what kinds of people would excel at which jobs.

I met a girl, in her early thirties, who had built a small chain of fashion boutiques. She was a total fashionista with the requisite Gucci shoe collection. I am going to refer to her as Shop Girl or SG. By the time we met, SG's stores had dwindled to one location. It was a pity because her stores were really fun and on-trend. SG had a great rapport with her customers—too cute and very charming. We had coffee and SG told me how she lost her stores and managed her business into bankruptcy. SG's final store would be closing soon and she asked me to offer her advice on a new career, becoming a buyer.

I pride myself on being a good career coach and a better judge of talent. By the time I met SG, I had counseled over 1,000 people from students to CEO's. Never did I see a worse fit than a buying career for a girl who had admittedly made so many mistakes in business. She would have made a great personal shopper, stylist or sales associate, I thought. I had no idea how to help her. SG told me she had an interview with a major retailer in the area. I told her what I thought she ought to do to prepare, but in my mind gave her no chance of getting a second interview.

You know in movies where something is about to happen to the main character and they fast forward through all the stuff you were expecting to see to get to a certain crescendo? Well, the next time I spoke to Shop Girl (which was about a week later), she'd been hired as a big time buyer for this giant retailer. What? Huh? What happened? Shop Girl had the Passion For Fashion and a great nose for trend-spotting and this giant retailer believed they could teach her the rest. They did, SG flourished and as a senior executive at this company she is one of my proudest misjudgments.

So, don't be too concerned when an old fart like me or somebody else says you can't do something. Personality and passion will often make up for some of the skills you may lack.

You Know You Are A Buyer If?

5- Suzy asks you if you like her jeans and you say, "Totally, but you should also get this top, this belt, that brown bag and those riding boots."

4- You have had your colors done.

3- You get mail almost exclusively from friends named Saks, Neimans and Bloomies.

2- Someone goes into your closet and asks you why you have like 10 pair of the same jeans. "Hello, they're all different."

1- Instead of collecting baseball cards, you collect cards from your aforementioned friends Saks, Neimans and Bloomies.

Cash And Path

Like most entry-level gigs, assistant buyers are not immune to a limited cash flow. An Assistant Buyer can expect to make between $18,000 -$35,000 per year. An Associate Buyer can make between $35,000-$70,000 per year. Buyers and Sr. Buyers can generate between $50,000-$125,000 per year. Divisional Merchandise Managers and Group Merchandise Managers can make between $150,000 per year and well over $1,000,000 per year! Top line salaries have dwindled a bit in the past decade and the big bucks are doled out at only the top retailers.

Assistant Buyer

Bone up on your Excel and PowerPoint skills. You will become the queen of the spreadsheet and prince of the presentation. At this level, you are making copies, keeping calendars for your boss(s) and taking notes. You are also attending buyer meetings, meeting with vendors and traveling.

Associate Buyer

This is a grooming level. When you reach this level, your bosses are trying to gauge if and when you will be ready for full-buying responsibility. You may get to develop private label product at this level. You may also get to take on some smaller buys and run your own buyer meetings.

Buyer & Sr. Buyer

You've really made it at this level. How proud will mom be when she is at the market and bumps into, Sherri, the mother of your high school nemesis and tells her that you are a hot shot buyer! One word, AWESOME!

At this level you should have full responsibility for buying your category(ies) and may be responsible for developing product, too. You have the responsibility now to use all of the analysis, margin info and trend info to purchase the right product for your stores. This is a big job no matter what the level. However, sinking your open-to-buy into bad product can be a fast track out the door. You have to be smart about what you buy and maybe more importantly, what you don't buy.

There can be a huge discrepancy in cash between buyers, even between buyers with the same experience. My friend Sue was the head accessories buyer for a small chain of luxury department stores. She had full responsibility for buying Marc Jacobs, Gucci, Chanel, Prada…all the luxe brands. She had almost ten years experience and she made less money than an associate buyer at Sears. Why the chasm of cash between buyers? It comes down to dollars and sense. If you are buying big volume, a lot of product, you are going to make more money no matter how inexpensive your product is.

DMM and GMM

When you have made it to this level, boy have you made it. Seriously, this is a job with a lot of perks. Yeah, you work and have a lot of responsibilities like managing your team of buyers, overseeing a gargantuan budget and staying on top of what's haute and baby, there are perks.

OTB-Defined:
OTB or Open-to-buy is a term that refers to how many free dollars you have to buy product. So, if my open-to-buy for season 3 is $12,000,000 then I can buy that much in goods.

Buying executives can generate monster salaries and often times have a large budget for travel and entertainment. After all, they need to know what's happening in their markets and offer guidance to their team as to what to target in their buys.

Super-Secret Backdoor Jobs

I am going to break down some of my Super-Secret Backdoor Jobs. They're not really a secret, but lack the sizzle that some of the other fashion jobs have. So, why discuss them?

Well, imagine you are applying for a design internship with your favorite designer. Is this designer just your favorite or do other people like this designer, too? Odds are if you are dying to work for someone then there are others willing to double-die to work for them. You could easily imagine that this design internship opening would be popular and at least 200 students might apply for this gig.

How you will get this gig we will discuss later. First, what I want you to learn is a simple truth about this industry—and many others. People hire people for their personalities. Are your skills important? Absolutely! Is your body of knowledge important? Totally! How about your willingness to work hard? Yes Yes Yes!!! Yet, hiring managers will also look to see if you have a certain vibe, aesthetic or "way about you" that they think will fit into a department or company culture.

I have a counter measure for this type of hiring practice. It's called GET IN THE DOOR. Go after all of the hot jobs you want, but if you find a company you really love, just get in! I believe 100% that once you get into a company, you can show them what you've got and move into other gigs once they've seen you are an integral team player.

These super-secret backdoor jobs are the jobs to consider as part of the Get In The Door plan. I am going to break them down into two categories, Retail and Fashion.

big time sidebar

Before I go on, I want to talk about retail jobs as a whole. Some people knock retail jobs and for someone that has proudly served hot wings (yes, I smelled like fried chicken all the time), sold men's undergarments and ladies shoes, I take offense to that notion. It is very important that at some time in your career you work in a retail store. First of all, the experience that you can gain in a retail environment will carry through to your whole career (more on this in the resume section). Second of all, having a retail job is like having a paid internship. Many big retailers have executive training programs or programs to go from a store to a corporate job. Many retailers look at their stores like training camps for the big leagues—their corporate jobs. They are looking for stars and stand outs. I know at least 100 guys and girls across the country that work 37.5 hours a week and make in excess of $100,000/yr. selling clothes in boutiques and department stores. I have friends that run your local Macy's that make over $150k and $200k/yr. I am not saying that you should pursue these jobs, but recognize that they do exist–I want you to keep your options open.

Retail Super-Secret Backdoor Jobs

There are a number of jobs related to buying jobs that most people get into as another option to the buying career You may have heard of these jobs already. Two of these jobs are Planners and Allocators. Another backdoor job is Product Development, an advent of vertical retailers and another spin off from buying jobs. So here's the real deal on these backdoor jobs.

Planner

First, let me start by saying that retailers are always scrambling to find planners and they pay top dollar for great planners. Simply put, planners plan what product should go into what stores. They have a financial job as they are analyzing numbers and making decisions about the flow and amount of product for specific regions and stores. You don't need to be an accountant to be a planner, but you need to have a good head for math and statistical data. Assistant Planners can expect to make between $35,000-$50,000 to start. Associate Planners and Planners can make between $50,000-$125,000. Directors of Planning can make between $125,000-$300,000 per year.

Allocator

Many fashion pros first work in the Allocations department before moving into Planning. Allocators partner with Buyers and Planners to analyze sales and allocate merchandise to stores. However, this is a job very few people actually go to school for and therefore has an easier entry-point than buying jobs and may be a spring board to a buying or planning job. An entry-level Allocator can expect to make between $30,000-$50,000. Sr. Allocators can make from $50,000 to $70,000 and managers of allocations can make in excess of $80,000 per year.

Product Developers

Because retailers can make the biggest margins off of product they make, whole departments have been created to manage the development of merchandise. Buyers grew out of just buying product into roles of developing product, from concept to delivery. They became creators of product, working with design teams and production teams. So, in this case the buyer who might also be a frustrated designer gets to fulfill that desire, to a degree. Product Developers can expect to make between $50,000 to over $90,000 per year.

The Super-Moist, Cakiest Job In the Retail World!

Ever heard of an RMM or Regional Merchandising Manager? This gig is a dream job. Most of these jobs exist in small numbers and just at the largest retailers. These Regional Merchandising Managers keep tabs on the product that goes on the sales floor. They consult with the buying teams to make sure the merchandise mix is right for each store in their region. They also develop relationships with vendors to create contests for their store associates and marketing opportunities for their region. So, how do you get this cake gig? Well, most people get promoted from the buying office or may even be former department store General Managers. These gigs pay between $90,000-$150,000. And yet, when you add the fun of going to fashion shows, traveling and the flexibility this job affords the salary may feel like $300,000 per year.

> When you add the fun of going to fashion shows, traveling and the flexibility that this job affords the salary may feel like $300,000 per year.

Super-Secret Backdoor Fashion Jobs

It takes a lot of talented people to create and produce product. The designer is just one of the many people who gives life to fashion goods. There are a couple of related jobs that are very key to the correct fit and construction of product that companies are willing to back up the money trucks for these talented pros. The two jobs I am talking about are Patternmakers and Technical Designers.

Patternmaker

Very few people go to school dreaming about being a patternmaker. This gig doesn't have the fashion cache many other fashion jobs have. But, I gauge jobs by their replace-ability factor. Are you easily replaceable as a designer, PR manager, or merchandiser? Yep. However, Patternmakers are one of the few positions in fashion companies that are super hard to replace. First of all, there are very few good patternmakers. Second, a good patternmaker is the difference between a well executed garment and total crap. They make the patterns for the production team or manufacturers to follow. Patternmaking is also one of the few jobs you can do in fashion where you can get steady work as a freelancer.

A few years ago, a patternmaker approached me to help her find a new job. She insisted that we meet ASAP! I had placed her in a job, but her former boss was aggressively trying to woo her back. She met me for lunch. Her English was so bad I had her repeat herself almost every sentence. She told me that her former boss offered her $150,000/yr. for 4 days a week of pattern services. I had just placed her in a job making $110,000 for an awesome company with growth potential (not bad for a Vietnamese Immigrant with four years experience). I told her she should discuss this with her current employer and tell them how excited she was about her career there. It was a risk, but the new company matched the old boss' offer and added on a very lucrative bonus structure. I had the pleasure of having lunch with her a year later. She picked me up from my office in her new fancy Mercedes and showed me her new freelance patternmaking operation. She makes about $200,000 per year working for herself about 30 hours/week. You know what I call that? Rad! Maybe I should ask her for a loan.

Technical Designer

Lots of patternmakers graduate into technical designer roles. Technical designers create the blueprints of designs for the production team or manufacturers to follow. They might also be the manager of the pattern department depending on the structure of a company. As a recruiter, I have had the hardest time finding competent technical designers. In major companies like Abercrombie & Fitch, Sears and Gap these technical designers have a very strong and fast career path. A technical designer with a couple years under their belt should clear at least $100,000/year if not much more. I have never quite understood why there aren't many more people clamoring to become technical designers, but again, it just isn't perceived as having the cache of some other fashion jobs. A step up from a technical designer is a position called a Director of Technical Services. This person is the manager of the Technical designer and pattern departments. This is a $200,000-300,000/year job.

Any day you check out the trades, read a paper or scour the net for fashion news, you will see a rumor or deal involving companies from outside of the industry. Big-time venture capitalists, high-digit investment funds and major companies from outside of fashion are gobbling up fashion companies and brokering mergers and acquisitions. There is a significant conglomoratization of fashion companies happening worldwide. What does this mean to the fashion job market? Well, that could be another book in itself, but some cool jobs are coming into the mix. Big consumer products companies like Johnson & Johnson, Procter and Gamble and Sara Lee have these neat jobs called Brand Managers.

And as these consumer companies keep coming into the business, these brand management positions are starting to flourish.

Brand Manager

You like marketing, love product, understand a bit of finance and sales. Then, brand management may be the job for you. Brand managers are the liaisons between these departments. They come up with the overall business plan for brands and ensure these related departments are executing the plan. This is a really neat and rewarding job in which you get to interact with many departments. This is definitely a job for someone with a head for business and advanced business degrees may be required. Brand managers can make $75,000/year while more senior brands managers can make well in excess of $150,000 per year.

The Super-Moist, Cakiest Fashion Job

My wife worked for a large fashion company and received these comprehensive and jaw dropping trend books. This company had a trend department that spent their time researching fashion trends in all categories. They talked color, culture and couture. They shopped the coolest stores and traveled to the coolest places. All of this work...um..fun, went into this amazing trend book. The director of this department had a very special and coveted position. There used to be a bunch of trend positions in the industry however, with shrinking budgets and the proliferation of companies like WGSN.com and other trend services, these jobs are dwindling. Still, that doesn't make them any less cool.

Director of Trend/Fashion Forecasting

Many years ago I worked on a search for a Vice President of Fashion Forecasting for Robinson's May (May Company's West Coast Dept. Store Chain, R.I.P.). In all the years I have looked for talented individuals for great jobs with great companies, no job has had as profound an effect on candidates as this one. Everyone wanted this job! I had people from major luxury companies begging me to help them get an interview with this conservative department store chain. This was an awesome job and the description read something like:

> *Travel to fashion shows, domestic and international*
> *Partner with buying teams on trend information*
> *Shop relevant markets for fashion-forward product*
> *Develop with executive product teams the seasonal concepts...*

In essence the job description was travel, buy stuff and report back.

This is the job of a Trend Director. Report to your creative teams what trends are breaking or going to break in the industry. Talk about competition in relation to a brands' offerings. Look, this is a great job for all of you out there with an eye for fashion who can't sketch to save your life. Expect to make $75,000-$150,000. Most often, these jobs go to designers.

A little Note About Styling, Wardrobing and Costuming

A lot of people ask me about styling, wardrobing and costuming. These are fun and often glamorous jobs. While I don't steer people from these jobs, I do offer some cautionary guidance. Most of the stylists, costumers and wardrobers that I know don't work year round (that's the nature of the biz) and don't work for one company. Rather, they work on contract, per project or freelance. The part that is really tough is how you budget yourself. You may not get reimbursed for your expenses for months and months. Besides the reimbursement part, these jobs can be very very fun and rewarding. I dated a stylist and got a lot of free clothes and hair care product. So, I am not complaining too loudly. If you become a stylist, costumer or wardrober, I am open to donations. I am a 42 Regular.

Other Jobs

If you are interested in learning about other jobs in fashion, check out the job lists in the back of the book for a quick description of loads of additional jobs in fashion.

Review

Whether you pursue a job in the fashion biz for love, for the money or both it is always nice to know your options. Keep in mind, a Plan B may be a good way to get your foot in the door. And remember, it is the "complete you" a company will end up hiring. Your passion, skills and your personality are a total package you will have to sell to get those great jobs. So, pick the jobs that mesh with who you are. You'll be on your personal path to cash and the better the fit, the more content you'll be.

Onto The Next Step:

Creating a resume everyone will love.

step two:
BUILDING A WINNING RESUME

I love resumes...I mean, I love good resumes. I could write an entire book just on the key elements that make a winning resume. So for this book, I will curb my enthusiasm a bit and give you the nuts and bolts view of resume creation and maintenance (yes, you also have to maintain a resume once you have written it).

Bond, James Bond

Your resume is a calling card. It tells the reader who you are and gives them a glimpse into both your qualifications and your attitude and aptitude. A resume announces who you are and what you can do for a company. When my favorite super spy introduces himself, you know his resume. If your resume is effective it will convey who you are with confidence and resolve as if you were 007 knocking on the HR Managers door...but without the accompanying supercar, $5000 tailored suit or gadgets.

More Weight

The good news is that most people, especially your competition, have bad resumes. These resume techniques are the simplest way to beat out your competition for an interview. So, the difference between you getting a job and the other 500 people applying for the same job may come down to what you write on one simple piece of paper. Now, let me add some weight to this bar and tell you that out of every resume that passes my desk, 98% are considered bad. Let's see, I look at 3000 resumes per week x 52 weeks=156,000 resumes. This means 3120 resumes are good resumes and 152,880 are just bad. There is no such thing as an okay resume; it is either good and effective or bad. And that is a staggering figure for such a simple task. So, let's put this fact to work in your favor.

What it do, Nephew?

What a resume does is spell out your qualifications to an employer, right? Well, that's what a bad resume does. A good resume highlights your successes. I know some people may disagree with me, but I offer this question: If you simply state your qualifications for a job, what will separate your resume from the hundreds of other resumes that simply state their qualifications? The answer I usually hear is, "The most qualified candidates will be called for an interview." OK, there is an opening for a store manager and you are submitting your resume for the job. This gig is for a hot store and you know a few people that are applying for the job. You work at a similar type of store and think you are a lock for the job. But, what about your buddies and the 50 other area store managers that will be applying for the job? Aren't they qualified? What are they going to put on their resumes? Well, they are going to put their job duties on their resumes just like you. So, I ask you, what makes you different? Why do I need to meet you? A good resume addresses these very questions—it says you *need* to meet me and here's why. So, just listing your qualifications does not effectively answer this question. You have to do more, put the total you on paper and frankly, that's what a good resume do, nephew!

The Anatomy of a Winning Resume

OK, so you know your resume details your experience. This is what a basic resume is, a detail of your experience. However, a winning resume is both art and science.

You Artisan, You

You are going to be an artisan, an artiste, a resume savant...put on your beret. The art part is a delicate dance addressing the details of the jobs and industry you target, without giving away too much info. Economy of words is very important when building a resume. You should try to get as much information across to your readers using the fewest words.

Example of a Bad Entry

> • Developed visual merchandising program for three district stores and the result of this program led to a successful holiday promotion that realized an increase in sales.

The above entry is bad because it is too specific and too long. It could be written with fewer words and have much more impact. In addition, it is always good to include numbers when relevant. Including a percentage of the increase in sales makes the entry concrete in terms of industry data and it also looks much more professional.

Example of a Good Entry

> • Developed visual merchandising program for the district that helped generate a 60% increase in sales.

The above entry is a good entry because it gives the right information. It says you can handle rolling out a merchandising program for a district (instead of just three stores). It says you can drive the bottom line through your visual efforts. It gives them numbers they like to see. It says you can effectively manage a team. It also says you are a star, not just a star for the holiday season. And, it says all of that with 12 fewer words. It is faster, more professional, more powerful and easier to read. It speaks their language.

The Secret of Writing the Artful Entry

Approach your resume entries in two stages. Think of your first try as a rough draft. Just explode all of the information you want onto the page and walk away. Then, come back to the resume and edit, edit, edit until the entry reads fast, powerful and easy.

She Blinded Me with Science

The glue or binding agent of your resume lies in the science of resume writing. I like formulas, you like formulas, we all like formulas. The formula for a winning resume is based on a grocery list. I am talking about your job entries. It helps to remember that what you will write and how you will write it has really already been recorded, even before you touch pen to paper. It isn't scary, daunting or hard. It is just a matter of recalling what you did at your previous jobs or internships in response to the great resume grocery list.

The Grocery List

When you build a resume, you have to include the job qualifications companies are looking for. Use job descriptions of jobs you like as a grocery list of things you need to have in your resume. It really is like making a great meal. If you are trying to make a killer meatloaf would you leave out the meat? So, when an employer is looking for candidates with MS Office proficiency, it better be in your resume, or they'll be moving on to the next one. Make sure you include all of the ingredients the employers are looking for. Treat these job descriptions as your grocery list.

To get started, pull a job description of a job you so want. For the sake of fun, I have pulled a job description of a job I like.

Design Director, Cool Clothing

Description:
- Execute and maintain the vision of the Creative Director
- Ensure the integrity of the Cool brand
- Recruit and develop design team
- Create management systems for design department
- Coordinate design calendar with merchandising and production teams
- Partner with Executive team on researching industry trends and sourcing market opportunities
- Source new vendor partnerships and evaluate current vendor programs against quality and price standards
- Direct photo shoots and all design-related promotions

Requirements:
- 7 plus years design experience with 3 plus years in a management role
- Expert understanding of knits, wovens, denim, accessories, intimates and outerwear for men and women
- Experience managing a team of designers, product developers, merchandisers, graphic designers and technical designers
- Knowledge of Action Sports Industry a must

From Job Description to Grocery List

I am going to turn this job description into a grocery list. This quiz will tell me all of the things I need to include in my resume to make it a winner.

First Item on The List...
❏ Are you a Design Director? (Can you be?)

Next Items on The List...
Job Description:

❏ Do you Execute and maintain the vision of the Creative Director? Have you?

❏ Do you Ensure the integrity of the brand? Will you?

❏ Do you Recruit and develop a design team? Can you?

❏ Do you Create management systems for the design department? Done it before?

❏ Do you Coordinate design calendars with merchandising and production teams? Well?

❏ Do you Partner with the Executive team on researching industry trends and sourcing market opportunities? Have you been there?

❏ Do you source new vendor partnerships and evaluate current vendor programs against quality and price standards? Got it?

❏ Have you Directed photo shoots and all design-related promotions?

Requirements:

❏ Do you have 7 plus years design experience with 3 plus years in a management role?

❏ Can you demonstrate an Expert understanding of knits, wovens, denim, accessories, intimates and outerwear for men and women?

❏ Can you explain your Experience managing a team of designers, product developers, merchandisers, graphic designers and technical designers?

❏ Do you have Knowledge of Action Sports Industry?

Shake and Bake

Okay, so you see what I did, I turned every duty or requirement of this job into a grocery list. Now, I have to answer in detail each question. If I can do this effectively then I will have a winning resume.

Look at how I use the ingredients on the list to make the job entries on this resume examples of successes:

XZ Company   2/2003-Present
Design Director, XZ Company

- Partnered with Founder/Creative Director to execute designs based on the company vision.

- Traveled to Asia, Europe and major US Markets to research trends, competitors and garner inspiration to ensure brand integrity.

- Recruited new staff of design and development personnel from contemporary stalwarts to continue the fashion-forward progression XY is known for.

- Created department operational manual as a tool for department cohesion and employee development.

- Launched Web PDM software to maintain calendar and streamline communications with design, production and overseas vendors.

- Analyzed business opportunities and licensing deals with Executive team. Developed $30 million private label business with Macy's.

AB Company   12/00-2/2003
Head Designer

- Lead new vendor sourcing that resulted in a quality increase and a 7% margin increase.

- Directed limited edition outerwear collection for Action Sports Retailer Trade Show celebrity press junket.

- Expanded collection from men's and women's knits, wovens and outerwear to include intimates, babies and accessories.

- Promotion resulted in managerial responsibility of design, pre-production and merchandising departments.

That was easy. In two job entries in this resume, I addressed what was asked of me. I used some artistry to address each ingredient with a bullet of success. Let's review.

First Item

Are you a **Design Director?** ☑ Yes. I answered this question with my most current job title.

Next Items…
Description:

Do you Execute and maintain the vision of the Creative Director? ☑ Yes. I worded this answer to make it clear I am a collaborator and executor of the Creative Directors' vision.

> • Partnered with Founder/Creative Director to execute designs based on the company vision.

Do you Ensure the integrity of the brand? ☑ Yes. I answered this question by also letting the reader know I travel overseas. Lots of design companies want senior personnel to travel overseas; it's always good to tell the reader you are well-traveled.

> • Traveled to Asia, Europe and major US markets to research trends, competitors and garner inspiration to ensure brand integrity.

Have you Recruited and developed a design team? ☑ Yes, being an effective manager requires that you can identify key talent for the job and develop them into superstars. I could have said that I had recruited staff, but I wanted the reader to know I can bring in the right staff for a particular environment.

> • Recruited new staff of design and development personnel from contemporary stalwarts to continue the fashion-forward progression XY is known for.

Have you Created management systems for a design department? ☑ Most design companies will not ask this questions, but I wanted to throw it in there because more and more fashion companies are becoming corporate. Management systems may be a key ingredient in your success. So, Yes, I included this example.

> • Created department operational manual as a tool for department cohesion and employee development.

Have you Coordinated design calendar with merchandising and production teams? ☑
Most larger fashion companies use web production and design management software. These programs are web-based programs that keep all of the necessary departments communicating and monitoring the design and production processes in real time. If you have experience with these types of programs, always put them in your resume. Yes.

> • Launched Web PDM software to maintain calendar and streamline communications with design, production and overseas vendors.

Do you Partner with Executive team on researching industry trends and sourcing market opportunities? ☑ Yes, I not only acknowledge I am a part of the executive team, but I also show how I am involved in the development of the company.

> • Analyzed business opportunities and licensing deals with Executive Team. Developed $30 million private label business with Macy's.

Have you Sourced new vendor partnerships and evaluated current vendor programs against quality and price standards? ☑ Yes, I addressed this and showed I understand what relationships I have and understand the importance of analyzing product and price from vendors.

  • New vendor sourcing resulted in a quality increase and a 7% margin increase.

Have you Directed photo shoots and all design-related promotions? ☑ Sometimes the marketing or merchandising pros will style and direct photo shoots. Here, I tell the reader I can put together a special collection and style a show.

  • Designed limited edition outerwear collection for Action Sports Retailer Trade Show and styled the line for celebrity press junket.

Requirements:

Do you have 7 plus years design experience with 3 plus years in a management role? ☑ I have answered this by stating the number of years of employment I have at a managerial level.

Can you demonstrate an Expert understanding of knits, wovens, denim, accessories, intimates and outerwear for men and women? ☑ Yes, I can show I have had full collection responsibilities since at least 2000. I also showed I had the background and gusto to expand into lots of categories.

  • Expanded collection from men's and women's knits, wovens and outerwear to include intimates, babies and accessories.

Explain your Experience managing a team of designers, product developers, merchandisers, graphic designers and technical designers. It is always great to talk about awards, accolades and promotions.

  • Promotion resulted in managerial responsibility of design, pre-production and merchandising departments.

Do you have Knowledge of Action Sports Industry? ☑ Well, if I used real company names, the reader should know by the names of the companies listed in my work experience, that I have worked in the Action Sports World. In addition, I mention the collection for the Action Sports Tradeshow.

In Summary

To sum up, I covered all of the questions asked in the job description. I also did so by making the answers real examples of successes and strengths. The result is a resume that is part art and science, simple and to the point. If I received this resume, I would be excited to meet this candidate because this resume would be better than at least 95% of the resumes I would receive for this job opening.

Anatomy of A Header

Don't Speed Past Your Header. Yeah, it's simple, but don't miss the opportunity to start off right.

Take a look at this resume header:

> ### Pat Reiter
> 32 Shell St. Laguna, CA 92222   949-789-5555 x102

What's wrong with it?

To answer this question, here's the checklist of things that need to be included in your resume header:

A) Your name
B) Your Address
C) A Private telephone number to reach you
D) A working e-mail Address

Now, what's wrong with the entry above? There are numerous issues and possibly some you can't see.

Your Name

Please don't laugh. Of course you know your name, but the reader does not. The name Pat or Chris or Sam could be used for either gender. If you have a name that falls into this category, put a Ms., Mr., Mrs. In front of your name. This way, when a hiring manager calls you, they know Pat is a guy and not a girl, for example.

> ### Mr. Pat Reiter
> 32 Shell St. Laguna, CA 92222   949-789-5555 x102

There is another part of the name game that can be a bit tricky. I have a friend whose name is Gene and he goes by his middle name, Trent. If you go by a different name other than your first name, put the name in quotes:

> ### Gene "Trent" Jones
> 323 Sawer Street Dana Point, Ca 02993 949-200-7000 tr@aol.com

Now, when a hiring manager calls Gene, they know he goes by Trent. A matter of taste comes into play when talking about nicknames. Often I see resumes with, what I call, cutesy names or street tags. This is *your* resume, I am just your guide, but when I receive a resume from a girl whose nickname is "Punkin" or "Cutie" I find it hard to take them seriously. If these names were their given names, well, that's a different story, but these are nicknames we are talking about. Nicknames like, "lil' Puppet", "Killa", "Ghost" and the like are equally difficult for me to call.

While it certainly isn't necessary, I always appreciate some phonetic help with more difficult to pronounce names. I hired a girl named Marsha. When I called and asked for "Mar-Sha" I was corrected by "Mer-Shay." I knew a girl named Amy, spelled Amie. Years later I knew another Amie, but she pronounced her name as "Om-ee-ay."

Amie "Om-ee-ay" Smith
2222 Jump St. New York, NY 10003 212-333-3333 am@it.com

Your Address

What is so difficult about your address? Seems pretty straight forward, right? Students tend to use their parents address, but what if the student lives in another state and intends to work in that area. Then, they should use the address that is most local to the jobs they are going for. Companies look for local candidates first and sometimes, exclusively. So, having an address that is local to a job is very important unless the company stated they will relocate employees. If you live in an area that is outside of where you are applying for jobs, but you intend to move to this new locale you can address this in your cover letter. I will get to cover letters, later.

Over the past several years people have become more sensitive about their personal information, and justifiably so. More and more candidates are using only their city, state and zip code as their address. I would prefer seeing the candidate's full address because a specific locale may be relevant to the job. But, if you feel you need to omit this information then at least give your city, state and zip code. I have no problem with people using personal mail boxes or post office boxes, but I would refrain from using business addresses…for obvious reasons.

Telephone Numbers

This cracks me up. Please, people, change your voice-mail message! I will run to see any Will Farrell movie, I love watching Crank Yankers and dumb stuff on You Tube, and although you may be able to burp for 40 straight seconds, which is impressive, I don't want to hear your feat when I am calling you about a job and get your voice-mail. I don't want to hear you sing. I don't want to hear a joke. I don't want to hear a murder mystery. And I certainly don't want to hear your unsigned band. I want to hear your name, a brief and cordial request to leave my name and number and that's it! Nothing else. And please please, keep it upbeat. If you sound like you just committed a felony, ran a marathon or lost your beloved cat, that's no good. Please compose yourself, put on your happy voice and leave a nice message.

I suggest you have a dedicated number, when searching for a job. This phone number is a place for people to leave messages about jobs. This number would not be your frat house, your grandma's pie shop or…your BUSINESS LINE. So many people use their business number as a number to get calls about jobs. I don't get it. You need to use a number on your resume where you are easy to reach and can speak, freely. If you can speak freely at work about another job opportunity, well that's unique. I know very few people who can openly talk about another great job while at their current not-so-great-but-is-currently-paying-my-bills-I-hope-they-don't-know-that-I-am-looking-for-a-new-job job.

A Working E-mail Address

"Working" means this e-mail address is active. I would even go further to say that your e-mail address should not only be working, but also permanent. I have resumes of candidates from 1998. What if I had a great job I wanted to tell them about, and let's say we had not spoken for 5 years. It's pretty likely their address has changed so my first attempt to contact them will likely be e-mail. If they've dropped their e-mail address, they may be out of touch. If you have a permanent e-mail address no matter where you go in the world, I can always reach you. Gmail, Yahoo and Hotmail all offer free permanent e-mail boxes. So, don't use your school e-mail which will be invalid in a few years. Don't use the work e-mail address of the job you are leaving unless you really want your boss to know you are looking. By the way, if you think your e-mail at work is private, you are 100% wrong. Your employer has the right to access your correspondence and files, anytime. And, please don't keep your resume in a file on your work computer.

And now for my favorite part of the e-mail address stuff. What are you trying to say with your e-mail address? Or rather, what does your e-mail address say about you? I have an e-mail address I set up through Gmail. It is **myname@gmail.com**. It isn't offensive, inappropriate or freaky. Some people have e-mail addresses set up just for job correspondence, which is a totally smart thing to do. When you log into your dedicated job search e-mail address, you should only see job stuff (and maybe some spam). That way you can easily manage and organize your job search. Please enjoy my top ten favorite worst e-mail addresses. These are real addresses I have seen in actual e-mails to me. I have changed the domains to protect the sort-of-innocent. Below I list some words and themes to stay away from in e-mail addresses.

The Top-10 Worst E-mail Addresses

10. **Biatchy@blank.com** – Got this one last year from a young designer.
9. **loverxxxoooforyouxxxooo@blank.com** – A girl handed me this one when I spoke at her school. I blushed when I read this address.
8. **needattention42@blank.com** – A resume of an aspiring actress applying for finance job.
7. **Imsooodesperate@blank.com** – A senior executive from an apparel manufacturer. Got her to change her address to her name.
6. **pillowfarts2@blank.com** – From a resume of an insurance broker. Who says insurance people don't have a sense of humor.
5. **Bloodkiller@blank.com** – A very sweet young design student whose name translated to blood killer in English. Got her to change her e-mail address to BK@blank.com.
4. **deathjunkie@blank.com** – Just weird.
3. **uhavebeeoh@blank.com** – How did he know? A resume of a young grad student.
2. **ihatemyboobs@blank.com** – An aspiring fit model, seriously!
1. **willwrk4sex@blank.com** – A resume I received for a senior level merchandising position. The resume was perfect for the job. I didn't even see the e-mail until a colleague I sent the resume to asked me if it was a joke. When she pointed out the e-mail address I realized it was a prank from a rival company. I got them back.

Refrain from using these words and themes in your e-mail address:

- Kitty or other cat derivative	- Princess (unless that is your name)	- Angel	- Killer or Killa	- Drunk
- Dog, Doggie or other derivative	- High Maintenance	- Devil	- XOXOXOXO	- Anything with "–oholic" in it
- Lover	- Curse Words	- Joker	- Kisses	- Dead
- Sex	- Beotch	- Anything violent	- Hugs	- Blood
- Sexy	- Hottie, Cutie, Gorgeous or Beautiful (really!)	- Anything illegal	- Drugs	- Terminator
- XXX		- Anything disgusting	- Any gas reference	- Dominator
		- Anything that boasts a private skill	- Pimp	- Slave
			- Beer	

Now That Your Header is Complete…

We need to focus on a piece of your resume that some feel they must put in and some don't. After reading tens of thousands of resumes in my career, I am anxious to get to the meat of your resume, your work and academic experience. For me, the Objective Statement isn't as critical. I know many professional resume writers and human resources pros that would disagree with me. You make the call.

Objective Statement

This is not a statement about your hotness or a note about your favorite objects or secret missions. This is a short statement (a sentence or two) about what your goal is in obtaining work. Simply, you are stating the kind of employment you are looking for in relation to your attributes for this kind of work. Here's an example of a typical Objective Statement:

> Objective: *To find a job where I can use my creative skills to grow within a company.*

What does this objective statement say about the writer? It doesn't tell me much except that the writer doesn't have a specific goal, job type or real skill set. Any good Objective Statement states a clear goal, a specific job path or job type and the skill set to execute a particular job. Here's an example of a good Objective Statement:

> Objective: *To leverage my expertise as a senior technical designer to help a contemporary collection expand into the luxury market.*

This Objective Statement is a good statement because it states a clear goal (technical expert for a contemporary company moving into luxury goods), specific job path (technical design department) and job type (technical designer). It also lets you know this candidate has experience in her field (Sr. Technical Designer). However, this Objective Statement may be too specific. What if the job she is applying for has nothing to do with the luxury market or the company is looking for someone less senior. Your goal, as always, is to give just enough information, but not too much. Remember, you can add, refine or edit your Objective Statement at any time. Make sure the statement is right for the specific job you are applying for. If it doesn't make sense, do some editing to make it work for the job you are applying for. Here is an example of a great Objective Statement:

> Objective: *To leverage my expertise as a technical designer to add to the technical team at a growing apparel company.*

I stated my experience without being too specific. I also talked about my goal and emphasized the team aspect (everybody loves that). As a bonus, I threw in a bit about working for a growing company. This lets people know I am ready to work and welcome the pressures and excitement of a company on the rise.

Your Experience

This is the super critical part of your resume. Your work experience says a lot about who you are as a person and more importantly, what an employer can expect from you as an employee. Below is a sample portion of a resume including **Work Experience** for your reference:

Amie "Om-ee-ay" Smith

2222 Jump St. New York, NY 10003 212-333-3333 am@it.com

Objective: Develop my skills as a fashion designer with a growing juniors design house.

Work Experience:

(1) Adam's Au Courant Apparel
(2) Los Angeles, CA
(3) Design Assistant   (4) 1/2007-Present

(5) • Developed prints for all graphic T's
   • Sourced new denim washes and novelties for SMU's
   • Created line sheets for sales, design and production staff
   • Produced 20-sku collection for Barney's Green Project
   • Solely responsible for tech pack creation for use with overseas vendors

---

The first thing you might notice when looking at the work experience entry is all of the bullets. Those bullet-points are important because they let the reader know you have written something important about your experience. You may also notice the economy of words. A lot of candidates want to write a lot. That is great, but the reader may not think so. The reader wants to read clean, precise, empowering statements about your experience. I took about 40 words to tell the reader I am an empowered and experienced Design Assistant. I also let the reader know my boss trusts me enough to charge me with the full responsibility of several aspects of design. That sounds like a winner to me.

Experience Job Entries By The Numbers

(1) **Company Name:** What is the company name, including dba's (if the company also goes by another name, include that).
(2) **Location:** List the City and State.
(3) **Title:** List your job title.
(4) **Dates of Employment:** List your dates of employment with month and year.
(5) **Experience Details:** Bullet-point your successes on the job.

I recently read a fashion employment blog entry where the writer penned their frustration about not getting many responses from their resume submissions. She exclaimed she would rather hire someone passionate who would work 14-hour days without experience vs. a 9-5'er with the experience, but not as much "passion." Someone posted a reply that read something like, "yeah, but the experienced one can get the job done in eight hours." Most companies want people who are up and running. They are flying and need someone to take the seat and fly with them. Training is time consuming and expensive. In the real world, you can have big company full of people with a lot of passion and no experience and that company would get very small very quickly.

So, make sure when you are filling out your experiences, you are telling the reader you (a) have the skills and (b) are ready to fly solo!

One quick note, if you have no experience and haven't had any jobs, what do you do? There is no substitute for actual job experience. Remember, Gap is always looking for fashionistas and fashionistos just like you! In fact, I know several people who started out working at Gap retail stores and now command six-figure salaries at Gap HQ in San Fransisco.

Your Education

Education is so important and if you are graduating and have done well in school, you may be inclined to write a small book on your academic prowess. I am totally cool with that except for one thing. Your resume should not be longer than a page and there are two other pieces you need to add before it is ready for its debut. I would like you to limit your educational listing to any schools you have graduated from to just your major and minor degrees (if you have a minor). If you attended any other programs like a study abroad program at a french art school, great, put that in. I am not a big fan of putting your GPA on your resume. I constantly receive resumes from candidates boasting a 3.2 or similar B average. That may not impress a hiring manager. I say leave the GPA stuff off and concentrate on making great job entries. Another thing I suggest you leave off is your year of graduation. Why? You never know what the hiring manager is looking for in a candidate. They may have an idea of an age range for a candidate (Disclaimer: discriminating against someone because of their age is a violation of state and federal labor laws…but, it happens) so, you don't want to be out of the running because you are too young or too old. Your goal is to just get your foot in the door. They can see how old you are when you are dazzling them with your skills and effervescence (yes, I just used the word "effervescence"…AWESOME!).

Education:
Adam's University, St. Louis, MO
BA, Apparel Design and Merchandising

It's pretty simple and straight forward, right? It is all you need for your education section.

Your Skills

This is such an important section of your resume and most overlook it. Rather, most omit it from their resume. If you were going for a buying job, wouldn't you want the hiring manager to know you use Excel, PowerPoint and other programs required for the job? If you were going for a design job, wouldn't you want the reader to know that you are a wizard with Illustrator? As a hiring manager myself, I want to know about your skills. If I am looking for someone with a particular proficiency in something and they don't list it, I pass on them. People, LIST YOUR SKILLS! But, don't list your hobbies (yes, I know you like movies and can ride a horse) and leave out your extra curricular skills (I am sure you are an awesome DJ, but I don't care). One guy listed as a skill that he could make a dollar out of fifteen cents. Then, why do you need a job? Although it was a silly entry, I did like the Tu Pac reference. (R.I.P. Pac). OK, I'm kidding! What I want to see are hardware and software skills, language skills, program certificates, etc., real world skills.

> **Skills:** Proficient in French and Spanish, conversational in Mandarin, proficient in Mac applications including Adobe CS4 and Quark Express.

Folks, that is it. If you take this process in steps, it is pretty easy. Again, remember your resume is a LIVING DOCUMENT; it should constantly change as your experience changes. You need to update, edit and work it for different jobs and scenarios. At the end of the book are resume templates for practice and some samples of simple resumes that work.

The Final Touch

References are required by many employers as part of their applicant screening process. Some candidates like to include their references on their resume. This is a mistake. Your references are fragile and important. A great way to lose a reference is to abuse a reference. Make sure only the most serious of circumstances merit access to your references. So, at the bottom of your resume, as your finishing touch write, **"References available upon request."** Then, the reader knows if they are really interested in pursuing you for a job, you have your references all lined up.

Check your own references

Read this carefully! Too many years ago, I was sewing up a deal to place a VP of Sales from Adidas at another major athletic brand. Let's call him, Jim. This guy was a fairly young hot shot. The placement of this candidate meant a lot of money to me; in my head I was already picking out my new Porsche. All I had to do was check this guy's references which were like a who's who list in fashion. It was tough to get through to most of his references because they were busy CEO's and senior executives. Some seemed irritated I was bothering them for their thoughts on Jim. Two references were luke warm reviews of Jim's skills and aptitude. The third reference was absolutely shocking! The third reference was from a lovely guy who initially had such nice things to say about Jim. When I asked him to rate Jim as a manager, he paused. He went on a rant about Jim's lack of management experience and his awful treatment of subordinates. He cited violent examples of Jim's office temperament and back stabbing. This went on for about ten minutes and then the reference told me he hoped he hadn't told me too much.

I went back and called the previous two references to see if they shared the same sentiments. It was like I said some magic word. They both torched Jim's ability to effectively develop and lead a team. Ethically, I had to share this information with the employer and they decided to pass on Jim. Bye bye Porsche. What's the rule here? Check your own references. Ask them the questions you think an employer might ask. If you don't like their answers, don't use them. In case you are wondering, Jim no longer works in the industry. It's a small world, my friends.

What if I don't have any work experience on my resume?

I am going to say a dirty word to many of you, brace yourself, hear it comes, okay, RETAIL! I cannot tell you how many people have come to me begging for a job in fashion, but refuse to work in retail. What's wrong with retail? Nothing! I worked retail for years and years. I learned about customer preferences, sell-through, merchandising and so much more! Want to learn your customer and build your resume, work retail!

How many jobs do you know where you can work 37.5 hours a week and make over $100,000 per year? I know a load of guys and girls who are professional sales people at Barneys, St. John's, Neimans and other luxury retailers who pull down huge bucks working a pretty leisurely 37.5 hours/week. I also know General Managers of your favorite department stores who pull down over $200,000 per year.

For many companies the store level is a proving ground for the next hot buyer, planner, visual pro and more. Many of the larger retail chains promote right from the retail floor into the corporate office. They may also have great executive training programs. They will literally pay you to learn different facets of their business, hoping you will be their next corporate exec. Pretty sweet, huh? So, you have no excuse not to try out a retail gig. It will be legitimate experience content for your resume and who knows, you may end up loving it. I sure did.

The Fast and Perfect Cover Letter

If a job description asks for a Cover Letter, then you must provide one. It's pretty easy to compose an effective cover letter. Here's what your Cover Letter should include:

1) The same header you use in your resume with your contact details.
2) The address of the employer and the name and title of the hiring manager, if applicable.
3) A short description of your experience and successes as it relates to the job description.
4) Include a mention about where and when you found the job ad.

Onto The Next Step:
Anyone up for some fun research?

Cover Letter Template
I have crafted an effective cover letter for you to peruse and use. It's in the back of the book.

back-of-the-book

step three:
RESEARCH

I can't tell you how much I hated school. My family called me the "text book underachiever", with good reason, too. I felt special. My momma said I was special so I believed certain things were going to just come my way. I am embarrassed to write this, but it is true.

I wish I had some awesome story about how I awoke from my lazy fantasy, but I don't have a great one. When I went to college, I went to a commuter college chock full of older students. My fellow classmates, in their forties and fifties, were taking a second shot at making something of themselves. I felt an innate sense of fortune and purpose. I had an opportunity to do something great with my life that these people had to wait for twenty or thirty years to start.

Things were easy for me. Math, science, reading, writing, listening, learning and most importantly, being in the moment, all seemed to be a purposeful part of me. It allowed me to fall in love. I really don't know what else to call it other than an obsessive love affair. I fell in love with research.

I am that guy who everybody knows that has resources. The guy that can get the tickets, get the deals, make things happen. Pure hustle, coupled with research and relationships made me *that guy*.

Being well researched is the key to many successes in life, especially in your career. Who would you rather promote in your company, the guy with the answers or the guy that doesn't have a clue?!
In order to be successful in landing great internships and jobs, you must be well researched.

Make It Happen Cap'n

I want you to know way more than your competition about fashion companies and the fashion employment landscape. Very few job candidates do the necessary research. It's sad, but true...and good for you. Do it and you'll have an awesome tool to land the best job for you. It's so easy; you can make it happen just as easily as some quick reads and fast notes. If you know where the jobs are and what companies are looking for, you are in a powerful position. Fashion employment research can be broken down into three groups for manufacturing/wholesale and retail:

> **Majors** - The big name companies
> **Competitors** - The big no-name companies
> **Undercovers** - The rest of the companies

I am first going to get into **Fashion Companies** (Wholesale and Manufacturing) and afterwards I'll talk about **Retail Companies**. Some of the information for these two sections may be redundant so you may want to pick just one section (the retail section or the fashion section). But, if you are simply falling in love with my writing, well, then press on through both. Hey, it can happen...I fell in love with research.

Majors

Most people want to work for the big boys because they are the brands everybody knows. But, if I ask you to name ten big Majors, it would take some thought. Research is about gathering information, analyzing it and storing it for use. Let's do some exercises. You will use the information you find in the following exercises as the foundation for your job search so really go for it. There are three main pieces of information I want you to extract when doing research on any company:

News, Facts & Figures -What's going on within this company?
Management -Who are the key players at this company?
The Senses -What is going on with this company's products/services?

Fashion Majors

Ralph Lauren, Levi's, Nike...these are some of the big names in fashion. How about some more big guys? Read this section carefully because I am going to have you start laying the foundation for finding a great fashion job using the following info. Let's do some research.

EXERCISE- Create Your Fashion A-List
The following information will help you understand how to research your favorite fashion companies. These are what I call, "A-List Companies." You can probably name a few A-List companies right now, but can you name ten companies you would love to work for? In the back of this book are worksheets for you to use in your research. Use the techniques that follow to start filling in the A-List Worksheet (in the back of the book) with 10 companies you would love to work for.

Work Sheet

Researching Manufacturers: A-List
Exploring cool brands is easy. All of the research is already done for you. Where do you find said research? Check out Adam's daily reads (There is a larger list of sites in the back of the book):

WWD.com (daily fashion news magazine-$)
WGSN.com (trend service with student rates-$)
just-style.com (daily global fashion news service–Free)
apparelnews.net (weekly fashion newspaper–Free)
net-a-porter.com (fashion mag and e-tail store)
style.com (Vogue's fashion portal–Free)
hintmag.com (fashion e-zine–Free)
stylehive.com (fashion shopping/social networking portal–Free)
thefashiontool.com (Check out our job board and see if you can find any companies that look interesting)

If you read these you will know your Libertine's from your Louboutin's in short order. Read about the brands mentioned in the same articles as your favorite brands. You will find some new cool companies for your A-List.

Fashion Majors News

Visit the websites of the companies you are researching. Go to the section of the site titled "Company News," "Company Info," "About Us" or "Press Releases." You may also find news information on the homepage. What you are looking for is news or interesting tidbits about the company, information the company wants you to read. Did they just launch a new product or service, hire a new executive or move into a new market? Write down little notes about the bits of news you find. You will use it later to blow these companies away, so make sure your notes are kept current and are legible.

Fashion Majors Management

Public companies will list their company officers on their sites. This information might be in the About Us or the Company Info sections. You are looking for two names to write in your notes. First, you are looking for the head of the company. This person might be a President or a Chief Executive Officer. The second person you are looking for is the person who would be overseeing your department. So, if you are a designer you want to find the Vice President of Merchandising or Executive Vice President of Design or a like title. If you are a marketing pro, you are looking for the Vice President of Marketing or similar title.

> Even though she had great references, gave a great first impression and had a winning resume she was not the right candidate for my team

You see where I'm going? Jot down this information in your notes and then do a search on them. Enter their name and company name and see if you can find any information on them. You are looking for company quotes about their products or services. You also might find information on where they have worked before and what groups or associations they belong to. More often than not, you will get a glimpse into these people, their vibe. This kind of information is interview gold!

Fashion Majors Senses

There is nothing worse than going into an interview without knowing what a company does, sells and makes. Several years ago I received a resume from a young lady who worked for one of my competitors. I interviewed her over the phone and she was on it. She said the things I wanted to hear; she was a performer and we knew some of the same people. She had the job if she wanted it. I had her come in to meet my team as a formality. I asked her what she thought and if she was ready to join us. She told me she liked the team and she liked me, but she needed to think about it over the weekend. I asked her to come back in on Monday. I had an offer ready to go. On Monday she came in and I asked her if she had any questions for me. She said she had just one. She asked me what our core business was. Oh, I was heartbroken. "My core business is the same as the core business of your current employer," I said. I asked her if she had ever heard of us and she said she hadn't.

Even though she had great references, gave a great first impression and had a winning resume she was not the right candidate for my team. After all, if she didn't know her competitors, didn't know how to research or worse, didn't care, what could she do for us? In my estimation, nothing. You have to know what a company is making, feel the products and research the service. Then, when you go in to meet these companies, you can speak intelligently about what they are doing. It makes you seem professional and invested and every company wants someone like that on their team. So, go check out the products of your A-List companies and take notes. Where is the product going? Is it moving more fashion forward? Is it denim driven? Has the fabrication changed? Turn yourself into a pro of their product.

Fashion Competitors

Here's where you become a sleuth, a detective, a modern day Sherlock Holmes. So, you have an idea who the big boys are, but you want to expand your list and read about other big boys. For instance, can you name the big Fashion Companies? There's Liz Claiborne and you probably know who they are. But, who are their competitors? Some of the big ones are Jones Apparel Group (Polo Jeans, Nine West, Anne Klein…), Vanity Fair (Wrangler, Earl Jeans, John Varvatos, Nautica), Kellwood (Enyce, Phat Farm, Sag Harbor, O by Oscar) and Phillips Van Heusen (Calvin Klein, Bass, Van Heusen). Did you know these other guys? They are huge and probably make some of the brands you love. How do you find out about the competitors of your favorite brands?

EXERCISE-Creating Your Fashion B-List

What's wrong with being on the B-List? Absolutely nothing. The Fashion B-List is your list of companies you are interested in, but don't know much about or companies you stumbled upon that look promising. I want you to find 50 companies for your B-List. Sound like a lot; it's not. Once you get started with the research, you will love it! Use the following info to get your "B" on.

Researching Fashion: B-List

First, where do you find them? Simple, you find them where they are looking for you! See, job boards aren't just for finding jobs. They are a premium source for research. To maximize your B-List try searches on a bunch of sites using different keywords. I have compiled a list of sites to peruse:

stylecareers.com	thefashiontool.com	monster.com
fashioncareers.com	theretailtool.com	hotjobs.com
allretailjobs.com	malakye.com	careerbuilder.com
fashionjobspro.com	retailjobspro.com	

Here's how you use job boards to find interesting companies. Do searches that match your interests. So, if I am interested in designing knits I would do a search for "Designer & Knits." What happens next is quite nice. You will see companies you are familiar with and also companies new to you. These unknowns have great jobs you are interested in, but is the company a good fit for you? Go to their websites and do some more research.

Another comment about using job boards for company research, often you will see e-mail addresses or names of recruiters and hiring managers to send your resume to. Write them down, you may want to use that information for your future job searches.

More research for your B's

Read the Wall Street Journal, read Women's Wear Daily. Subscribe to daily fashion news publications like Fashion Wire Daily or Just-Style.com. When you see a story about a company you don't know, look them up. I read these publications everyday and it takes me about 30 minutes to cover them. Friends and colleagues think I am really in the know because I can speak somewhat intelligently about the big news in the biz. That 30 minutes a day makes me sound like an industry pro and the information I use is also available to you. Often, I want to know in depth information about a company. I want to know news about a company, the executives who work there and the company's competitors. I use Hoovers.com as my number one tool in gathering company intelligence. This is mainly a paid service, but with a very limited free component. They do have student memberships and your school may already have access to Hoovers. Once you get the hang of using it, you will love it because of all of the in depth intel you will get. They have a cool feature that allows me to type in the name of a company and then access a list of its major competitors. If you type in the ten big companies you researched and maybe a couple more you found reading the trade publications, you can create a list of a hundred big companies in no time.

OK, you did your exercise and now you have your A & B-Lists. Nice! Let's move on for the final step of fashion research.

Fashion Undercovers

Who wants to work for a company they have never heard of before? The answer may be you. There is so much fierce competition to work for the haute company du jour that many of the lesser-known fashion companies get overlooked. And less competition means better odds of getting that awesome job.

EXERCISE: Creating Your Fashion C-List
You picked up 10 Fashion A-List companies, 50 Fashion B-List companies and now it's time to throw it into 5th gear. I want you to use the information below to find 40 Fashion C-List companies. We are going to use all of this research in the next chapter. Your good work here is laying the foundation for getting your resume in the hands of the right people.

Researching Fashion: C-List

Who really made the shirt you're wearing, those jeans you're rocking or those sweet sandals? That's a great question, usually, with some surprising answers. If the label on your shirt says Armani Exchange then Giorgio Armani must have made it, right? Nope. Lots of great product is manufactured by companies whose names don't match the name on the label. Sometimes this is because the product is licensed. Licensing a product means company A is a brand that sells the rights to manufacture and distribute under its name to company B.

Other times, product is just produced by a manufacturer other than the name on the label. These manufacturers may also have full design and merchandising teams. So, they can easily sell finished products for company A to slap a label on and voila, your new Armani Exchange Jeans are born! These manufacturers present a unique, fast-paced environment full of variety. Because, instead of just working on one brand, they might be working on 20 brands. So, how do you find these behind the scenes players? It's as easy as digging in your closet and sitting down at a computer.

I have a little game for you. Pull five pieces of clothing you love from your closet (tops, bottoms, jackets). Now, who makes those garments? Is it the brand on the label or someone else? The odds are that somebody else manufactures the garments you love. How do you find out? The Federal Trade

RN-Defined:

An RN is a registration number given by the government to identify manufactured goods. At www.ftc.gov/bcp/rn click "RN Database-Search" and select "RN" in the "RN type" field. Enter the RN and click "find." That's it. You don't need to fill in any other fields.

Commission has a website that allows you to find out who makes a particular garment by typing in a company's **RN**. RNs can be located on the back of a garment's tag. Then search for who the number is registered to at www.ftc.gov.

For Instance, let's say that you wanted to be a denim designer for The Limited. You applied numerous times and got nowhere. Why not try to get a gig designing denim for one of their biggest manufacturers? Type in the RN for your Limited jeans and Tarrant Apparel might pop up. Tarrant is a $500 million dollar **private label** denim manufacturer that makes many of denim bottoms for The Limited and others. They take the product from design through production. Now, you can thank Uncle Sam for the cool research tool. Your tax dollars at work finding you work. I love it.

Private Label-Defined:
Private Label is the term used for garments produced by one company for another company's brand.

Your RN research can lead you to some of these great Undercover Companies and that may be a very easy first foot in the door.

Retail Majors

Hot Topic, Saks Fifth Avenue, Foot Locker, Express and Macy's we know of, but what about the other big guys. Many of the giant retailers are merging or being acquired so it is extra important to be on top of these guys so you can speak intelligently about them. Let's retail research.

EXERCISE- Creating Your Retail A-List
The information below will help you figure out how to research your favorite retail companies. These are what I call, "A-List Companies." Can you name 10 hot retail companies? In the back of this book are worksheets to jot down notes about your retail research. Write down and research 10 companies for your Retail A-List. We will use this information later to get you that great gig.

Retailer Research: A-List

Having trouble coming up with ten retailers? Maybe I can turn you on to some reading material that might broaden your scope. Check out Adam's List of Retail Reads:

WWD.com (daily fashion news magazine-$)
WGSN.com (trend service with student rates-$)
just-style.com (daily global fashion news service–Free)
apparelnews.net (weekly fashion newspaper–Free)
net-a-porter.com (fashion mag and e-tail store)
style.com (Vogue's fashion portal–Free)

hintmag.com (fashion e-zine–Free)

stylehive.com (fashion shopping/social networking portal–Free)

WSJ.com (The Wall Street Journal–Free & $)

CSGIS.com (This is a retail directory, but they have good free downloads)

NRF.com (National Retail Federation offers solid news services–Free)

visualstore.com (A visual merchandising portal with good news and a nice message/job board–Free)

theretailtool.com (Check out our job board and see if you see any companies that look interesting–Free)

Everyday something is written about retailers. So, you can also use your local paper as a research source.

Retail Majors News

Visit the websites of the companies you are researching. Go to the section of the site titled "Company News," "Company Info," "About Us" or "Press Releases." You may also find news information on the homepage. You are looking for news or interesting tidbits about the company, information the company wants you to read. Did they just launch a new product or service, hire a new executive or move into a new market? Write down little notes about the bits of news you find. You will use it later to blow these companies away so make sure your notes are kept current and are legible. Also, check out business market sites like edgar-online.com and marketwatch.com. When you type in a retailer's name, you may get some juicy bullets of news on the company.

Retail Majors Management

Public companies will list their company officers on their sites. This information might be in the About Us or the Company Info sections. You are looking for two names to write in your notes. First, the head of the company. This person might be a President or a Chief Executive Officer. The second person you are looking for is the person that would be overseeing your department. So, if you are a buyer you want to find the Vice President of Merchandising or Group Merchandise Manager/ Divisional Merchandise Manager or like title. If you are a PR pro, you are looking for the Vice President of Public Relations or Vice President of Communications. You see where I'm going? Jot down this information in your notes and then do a search on them. Enter their name and company name and see if you can find any information on them. You are looking for company quotes about their products or services. You also might find information on where they have worked before and what groups or associations they belong to. Also, check their name with online networking sites like LinkedIn. More often than not, you will get a glimpse into these people, their vibe. This kind of information is interview gold!

Retail Majors Senses

There is nothing worse than going into an interview without knowing what a company does, sells, makes. I worked with Jones Apparel Group and I had known a senior executive at one of their big brands. This lady, "Judy", was a creative type and came in to different retail brands to rejuvenate them. She had an awesome pedigree, a world class resume of experiences (mostly at the luxury level). Years later I thought about her for a position with a major contemporary retailer. I talked to her about the position I was trying to fill with this big retailer. She didn't ask me many questions and agreed to go meet with them.

After her interview I got a call from the President of this $500 million retailer. She said she just had a very interesting interview with Judy. She told me they were impressed with Judy's skills, but had a question for me. I assumed they wanted to know if they could afford her since the President seemed very impressed. She asked me if I knew Judy had never been in their stores or seen their product. I was so embarrassed. How could someone so successful in the biz not know this big retailer? Better yet, why didn't she go visit one of their stores? But more importantly, why hadn't I asked her questions that pertained to this retailer before she went on the interview? I was dumb and so was Judy. I learned a valuable lesson that day about screening each and every candidate, thoroughly and Judy learned… well, she didn't learn much; they hired her, anyway. So, there are exceptions. Or, are there?

Three years later our paths crossed again. This time, I sent Judy for another job and she didn't get it. Why? Even with my best efforts to get Judy to research this new retailer, she didn't do it and as a result, didn't get the job. You have to know what a company does, feel the products, research the service. Then, when you go into meet these companies, you can speak intelligently about what they are doing. It makes you seem professional and invested and every company wants someone like that on their team.

So, go check out the stores and the products they carry. What message are they trying to convey in their windows, through their displays? Is the store moving more fashion forward? Is it executing a promotion or theme? Turn yourself into a pro of their stores.

Retail Competitors

There are so many retailers out there. Now, with the online retail explosion it seems a new hot e-tailer opens everyday. You probably have leftover companies from your A-List research, so lets put it to good use.

EXERCISE-Creating Your Retail B-List
Bcbg, Barney's, bebe, these are all "B" retailers, but are they on your B-List? You can use any retailers you like to build your B-List of 50 retail companies. These companies should be companies that you either have an interest in their products or the way they conduct business. Get to work!

Work Sheet

Retailer Research: B-List
Simple, you find them where they are looking for you! See, job boards aren't just for finding jobs. They are a premium source for research. You will have to try searches on a bunch of sites using different keywords. I have compiled a list of sites to peruse:

stylecareers.com	thefashiontool.com	monster.com
fashioncareers.com	theretailtool.com	hotjobs.com
allretailjobs.com	malakye.com	careerbuilder.com
retailjobspro.com		

Here's how you use job boards to find interesting companies. Do searches that match your interests. If I wanted to buy apparel I would do a search for something like "Buyer & Juniors" or "Buyer & Men's." What happens next is quite nice. You will see companies you are familiar with and also companies new to you. These unknowns have great jobs you are interested in, but is the company a good fit for you? Go to their websites and do some more research.

Another comment about using job boards for company research, often you will see e-mail addresses or names or recruiters and hiring managers to send your resume to. Write them down, you may want to use that information later.

OK, forget for the moment that you may be using all or some of these companies as employment prospects. Let's just look at your research so far as an exercise of knowledge. When a candidate comes into my office and they start talking about fashion companies and retailers and I mention companies, it is important they know what I'm talking about. If they don't know the difference between Marshalls and Marni, it hurts their credibility. Succeeding in this employment market entails that you know who the players are.

Retail Undercovers

This may be my favorite list of companies because it is the Retail Undercovers that take the most chances. They have to be different to survive and many of these shops are strictly awesome! I hope you delight in researching these gems and if you find a retailer you think rocks, e-mail me about it so I can visit them.

EXERCISE: Creating Your Retail C-List
You researched 10 Retail A-List companies, 50 Retail B-List companies and now let's put you over the edge. I want you to use the information below to find 40 Retail C-List companies. After you complete this, in the next chapter, we will start planning your attack to get your dream job.

Researching Retailer C-Lists
It's so easy to compile lists of cool retailers because, if you're like me, a mall rat, then your fashion research is your passion. Friends, I am talking about shopping. At least half of this book was written on a bench, in a comfy chair or at a food court table in local malls. I like the energy of people shopping, at least, that's what I tell my friends. The truth is I have two obsessions, eating junk food and shopping for shoes. Malls service my issues quite well. Enough about me, let's talk about you and your list of C companies.

Your C-List is a list of companies that you will probably find through fun discovery. Maybe you don't know these retailers or maybe you have seen them, but never given them much thought. Your first research assignment here is to go to your local mall. Pick up a mall directory, check out all of the stores. Did you find any stores that merit further discovery? Take your directory home and do some net research. If you didn't find any new and interesting stores at your local mall, shoot for a bigger pool to swim in. People, I am talking about the 900 hundred pound gorilla, the shopping planet... The Mall of America. Visit www.mallofamerica.com and see what Minnesotans are buying at the biggest mall in America.

I want you to try something else. Let me throw some names at you and see if you recognize them: Smith & Hawken, American Girl Place and Red Envelope. Retailing isn't just about clothing, of course. Garden Furniture, Dolls and Gifts all have thriving retail channels of distribution. The three companies I named are companies I think have interesting business models for retailing. They also present some really interesting opportunities for buyers, planners, field management and other corporate jobs. Consider adding some of these non-apparel retailers to your C-List of companies. Need to spark some ideas? Go back to your job board searches and do blank searches for retail and see what companies pop up that pique your interest.

It amazes me how many great smaller retail chains there are. Intermix, American Rag, Calypso, The Closet, Scoop, Reiss (US), and Madison are small chains my wife shops. Because they are small, they can pick up lesser known brands and niche products you might not otherwise find at Bloomies, Neimans and Saks. These Retail Undercovers are great for resume building because there is a shorter path to the front office and you get exposed to lots of different areas of the business. This does not hold true at most of the larger retailers. The bigger the retailer, the more numerous the layers. This means a more defined and usually more narrow job scope.

Need more research? Check out your local big bookstore and look for the travel magazines with names of cities on them, for example, Vegas Magazine, Philadelphia Magazine and Santa Barbara Magazine, etc. These magazines will often feature their own local retailers with insights into the vibe of the stores and may also feature contact information. Of course, your favorite fashion mags will also feature cool stores. Another way to search for interesting Retail Undercovers is to see who your favorite brands are selling to. This is research in reverse. Go to your favorite brands' web site and click on their Stores links to see which stores they sell to in a particular area, region, etc. See stores or chains you have never heard of? Check them out!

The Lists

What was up with all the lists?! You're going to use these lists to find your next job and hopefully keep these lists as you build your career. Now that your lists are coming together, let's work on you a bit.

Building Your Tool Belt

My Story

It sounds clichéd to me because I say it so often, but finding work *is work*. All your boys or your girls are having fun after class and you want to join the party. I get it; the last thing you want to do is go to work. This is especially true if you have a job. What really stinks is when you get out of school and you think you are going to get a really cool fashion job and you don't get any calls. Six months pass and you still don't have a job. The thought of being unemployed scared me a bit when I was in school because my mom really scraped by to make ends meet. I didn't want to be a burden on her after college so, I dedicated myself to preparing for my real career. After my part-time job and studying commitments were satisfied, I focused on things that would ready me for life after academia.

I wanted to be a writer at the time. I read books about writing and dedicated myself to making contacts in the entertainment industry. I took some writing classes after school and tried to dedicate myself to writing a screenplay every 2 months. Okay, that was ambitious. The funniest part about my desire to be a writer is that even though I had all of these great ideas, it was tedious to sit down and dedicate two hours a day to write. I would make deals with myself to write. For instance, if I wrote for 30 minutes, I could watch TV for 30 minutes. Or, if I committed myself to writing all day on Sunday, I could screw around the rest of the week. None of the deals I made with myself ever worked. What I figured out was that I loved doing what I loved doing. I loved meeting with and listening to professionally writers. I became very adept at networking and learned to keep a small pad of paper with me at all times. When I would get inspired, I would write in my note pad. By the time I graduated college, a few things happened. One, I had sold my first television show (for pennies, literally), completed an entire screenplay and learned how to network. I networked so well that I met people in other industries, namely, fashion. Soon, my interest in fashion overtook my interest in writing. My extra curricular work put me on the fast track for my first fashion industry jobs. It was work, all that writing stuff, but I enjoyed it and it set up the habits I used to launch my career.

So, how does my story relate to you? It does In a couple of ways. First, if you feel a sense of urgency about your career then you have the motivation to do something to really launch yourself. Second, if you decide to invest now in your career, you can really get an edge on the competition. Third, if you put yourself out there now, meeting people and starting business relationships instead of waiting until you graduate, you will be far ahead of the pack. Finally, you need to understand who you are and develop a way to build your skills that works for you.

Build Some Skills

Read a job description for a job you totally want to get when you get out of school. What does the job require as far as qualifications? Do you need to be proficient in Excel? Do you need to have flat sketching ability? Do you need to be able to create CADs?

Hone the skills in the job description as if it were a checklist of things to do. My wife read a job description for a job at Mossimo when she was going to school. After school and after her retail job she would spend hours in the computer lab sharpening her Adobe Illustrator skills. She only had one class in Illustrator and knew it was a complex program. So, she dedicated her free time to learning tricks from pros online and meeting people who were proficient in this program. She landed an interview with Mossimo as she was graduating and showed them a thick portfolio of bodies and sketches she had done on her own to build her portfolio. They were blown away and she got the job.

> *The first thing I tell everyone breaking into the business is learn Illustrator. The first thing I look for from a seasoned design pro is their command of Illustrator. I only hire Illustrator pros; I can't afford not to.*
>
> **Kristin Reiter,**
> **Design Director**
> **RVCA**

Like I said above, the answer to what skills you will need to get the jobs you want are in the job descriptions themselves. But, let's investigate some skills I think are paramount for your job quest.

Some Retail Skills

In my description about what a buyer does, you read that buying is a business job. It takes a business head as well as a fashion sense. First, let's look at some of the business skills. Your school probably offers some basic business classes where you will have to employ some use of Microsoft Word, Excel and possibly PowerPoint. Besides learning some basic analytical skills in these classes, knowing how to formulate, organize and analyze raw data is important. These MS Office programs help you do that and are tools that you can work on to become efficient.

Ace This!

How good is your software knowledge? This short quiz will tell you.

1) Microsoft Excel is?
   a. Chump
   b. A Word Processing Program
   c. A Grecian Formula
   d. A Spreadsheet Program

2) In MS Word, you can insert hyperlinks. What is a hyperlink?
   a. A passive link in a document
   b. An active link to a web page
   c. A Neanderthal hooked on sugary cereal
   d. An electrified fence

3) PowerPoint is a program that allows you to:
   a. Create Visual Presentations
   b. Code Google Algorithms
   c. Interact with animals
   d. Chart a course using your index finger

4) In Excel, which do you press to enter the current date in a cell?
   a. Ctrl + ; (semicolon)
   b. Ctrl + Shift + : (colon)
   c. Ctrl + your + temper
   d. Ctrl + F10

5) In order to save an existing document in Word with a different name you need to:
   a. Retype the document and give it a different name
   b. Ask it nicely
   c. Copy and paste the original document to a new document and then save
   d. Use the Save As command

6) In order to create columns in Word you need to:
   a. Press the space bar until your cursor reaches the desired place
   b. Kick it ol' school with a ruler and pen, word
   c. Tab consecutively until the cursor reaches the desired place
   d. Go to the Format menu and select Columns

7) In Excel, how do you change width in a cell to fit contents?
   a. Double-click the boundary to the right of the column heading
   b. Single-click the boundary to the left of the column heading
   c. Use pliers
   d. Press ALT and single-click anywhere in the column

8) In PowerPoint, how do you move an existing text box?
   a. Select "Edit" and "Cut" and then "Edit" and "Paste"
   b. Shake your computer until the text box moves to desired location
   c. Press F1 to select and then move the box with arrow keys
   d. Click on the edge of the box and move to desired location

9) What is the quickest way to start your own PowerPoint presentation?
   a. Draw it first and then scan it
   b. Click "File" and then "New" and follow the instructions
   c. Use the "auto content" wizard to produce an original design
   d. Select "Blank Presentation" then the blank sheet of paper, then OK

10) In Word, which keyboard shortcut bolds selected text?
   a. File/Format/Bold
   b. Bold Button
   c. Ctrl+B
   d. Alt+B

So, did you ace the quiz? Check your answers in the back of the book.

Microsoft has great quizzes and help for their programs on their website. You can use this link to get to their MS Office quiz page: **http://office.microsoft.com/en-us/help/ FX100485331003.aspx**

Board the Trends

Remember the story I told you before about the girl that wanted to be a buyer, but didn't really have the business skills? Well, the one thing she was great at was putting together trend boards. A trend board is a collage of pictures, text, swatches and other materials that illustrate a particular trend or an overall picture of trends for a category/market. Your fashion design department probably has a class that includes the creation of trend boards. These boards are helpful tools in visually defining a progression in the category/market that you want to convey. Many of the ones I have seen look like fashion vomit on a giant piece of poster board. Some had an innate sense of flow and conclusion, but only a few explained to me, in very defined terms, where a market was heading and served as a powerful medium for delivering a ton of info with so few words. Of course, it's all a bit subjective. Make some boards for your portfolio and ask your friends and colleagues what they think.

How is Your Portfolio Form?

The scariest moment in my career was also the funniest. I met a young fashion grad, Leah, that had a portfolio she wanted to show me. Her look was mall goth–an original Hot Topic shopper. She told me her portfolio was very Calvin Klein, clean lines and sophisticated silhouettes. Then, she began to take me through her flat sketches. The first sketch was of a Gumby green ball gown that was cut in two pieces. I asked her for a little more explanation since the torso of the girl in the sketch was not attached to her bottom half. She said, "Duh, she was sliced in half at a dance." I suppose I should have realized that from the liberal use of blood splatter. Each page was gorier and gorier. It was the worst horror movie I had ever been to and the scary part was I was in this girls' house, sitting on her couch, alone and frankly, scared. She got agitated as she could see the horror on my face in place of the jubilation she anticipated.

I told her I appreciated her book, but asked if she had anything to show me without blood and dismemberment. She rocked back and forth nervously and then bolted off the sofa giggling to another room. I had my chance to escape. Maybe it was my own morbid curiosity that kept me on that couch; maybe I was just paralyzed with fear. I sat and waited. She returned, shortly, with a sketch of a gown. No blood, no severed body parts were evident. It was, in a word, breathtaking. It was a vintage Halston-like dress I could imagine Gwen Stefani wearing to the Grammy's. It was a really sophisticated sketch. I asked for more. She told me that it was the only one she had and she did it because she was bored. She let me leave after I offered a few pieces of advice. I left scared, confused, relieved and totally perplexed.

Many times over, in my career, I have had milder versions of what I refer to as bad portfolio form. Who is your portfolio for? Is it for you, your friends, potential employers or the story boards for the new Halloween sequel? No. Your portfolio should be something employers can understand. It needs to show your art skills, your conceptual development and your aesthetic. It needs

On Portfolios

As a designer, your portfolio is the best evidence of your work. It's the key that will unlock opportunities, so make your portfolio the best representation of you! The "deal makers" in a portfolio are sharing some of your inspirations through a great mood board; fabulous illustrations, both by hand and computer-generated or computer enhanced; and a group for each season, including illustrations, flats, and fabrics/trims. The "deal breakers" in a portfolio are incomplete work, fabric samples that aren't neatly pinked (really!), and typographical errors in any of your text. About the portfolio itself: I highly recommend investing in a good black portfolio which can open up on a desk without having to clear anything off the desk. 14" x 17" is a good size. Avoid making a radical statement with the cover–not everyone is going to like pink fake fur.

Marianne Hudz
Former Director of Career Services
Otis College of Art and Design

to be cared for and updated, edited and expanded. The only thing the Leah portfolio showed me was a very brief glimpse of genius in a sea of dark silliness.

The Leah Rule

If you don't have a giant portfolio, what are you waiting for? Don't count on your professors to help you build your portfolio, you do it. Build your portfolio around the Leah Rule. The Leah Rule states that you must build your portfolio in a way that best showcases your abilities in art, concept and aesthetic from the viewers point of view. So, if someone looks at your portfolio and is scared by it, thinks it's too silly or dark or doesn't emphasize the three components above, you need to fix it or nix it.

If You Build It, They Will…

If your portfolio is easy to carry around, then you need to add to it. It should be heavy, full of awesome stuff. This is your calling card in an interview. If it's six pages of sketches and a line sheet then it's not screaming, "Winner Winner, Chicken Dinner!" You need a winning portfolio and here's how to build it. Pick five of your favorite designers and jot them down on a note card you can see when you sit down at your desk. These five designers are your portfolio projects to visit in your down time.

I will pick English sartorialist, Paul Smith for this example. I love Paul Smith's distinct design aesthetic. His designs are usually watered down, copied and manufactured by some of the big names in fashion in the US. For my portfolio builder project, I am going to translate Paul Smith Men's Sportswear for Fall 2010. I am going to concentrate on developing five looks that will include knit tops, woven bottoms and outerwear. Five Complete looks, fifteen different pieces, including a color palette and maybe even fabric swatches and trims. I would continue with four other recognizable fashion brands.

An Excellent Online Training Website: Need to learn these applications? You can access excellent video-based training at www.lynda.com. A $25 fee buys you unlimited training for one month.

Now, I added serious weight to my portfolio, showing a full range of skills. Employers can really sink their teeth into that. You need to just keep adding and adding to your book. Once you have enough material, edit your portfolio to ensure the employers that you show it to will understand it. It must make sense for their vibe and market.

Illustrator and Photoshop

Now, I am not sure where you are going to school, if you have gone to school or have never been. But, I can assure you one thing, if you want to be a designer or work in a design-related function you better invest some serious neurons into learning these programs. Again, Illustrator in particular, is the design program made by Adobe that is *the* tool for the biz. If we ever meet, I will quiz you about rasters and other Illustrator goodies. If you don't know what I'm talking about, get crackin'. Odds are there is a class at your school or a community college to give you the basics. You can also find training on the web. However, if you want to blow through the interviews and land great jobs, you better understand Illustrator and be able to use it expeditiously.

How do you know when you know enough? You never will, there are so many cool tricks, shortcuts and fun finds in this program. It is just awesome. When you are good at it, it's like, for me, watching a master cellist or concert flautist. It is an art, for sure.

A Quick Note on Portfolios

I see a lot of design portfolios. Nine times out of ten I ask the candidate if they have more to show me. A few tears and some freehand sketches don't give me the big picture of who you are as a designer and what you can do. I want to see your range. The response I usually get when I ask for more is usually something along the lines of, "well, this is what I have." Often young designers have smaller portfolios because they haven't had a lot of real work experience. That's lame. You have no excuse for not having a great book with lots of depth. You don't need ten jobs to have a thick portfolio. Building your portfolio is so easy. Like I mentioned before, just challenge yourself to design future seasons of your favorite designers. You give yourself the projects and give it all you've got.

Online Portfolios

Set up your portfolio online and include a link to your portfolio in your resume header or footer. This is an easy way for hiring managers to check out your stuff. **creativehotlist.com**, **styleportfolios.com** and **coroflot.com** are just a few portfolio sites that are free to use.

Are You Illustrious With Illustrator?

A quick beginner's test just to keep you in check:

1) Another name for a raster image is:
 a. A bit map
 b. A pixel map
 c. A photo of a Jamaican Dance Hall
 d. A graphics map

2) Bitmap images are represented by:
 a. Pixels
 b. Paths
 c. Cheese
 d. Nodes

3) When you want to smooth the appearance of pixel-based lines, objects, and text, you would use:
 a. Aliasing
 b. Interlacing
 c. Anti-aliasing
 d. A brick

4) How many colors are included in the Web-safe, or browser-safe, color palette?
 a. 300
 b. 216
 c. 256
 c. 14

5) The command used to permanently change the size and resolution of an image in most graphics software is called:
 a. Resample
 b. Cut
 c. Zoom
 d. Crop

6) Opening a vector image in a bitmap editing program will cause the image to become:
 a. Corrupt
 b. Scary
 c. Pixelated
 d. Rasterized

7) When scanning an image for screen display only, the final resolution should be:
 a. 300 dpi
 b. 72 ppi
 c. 600 dpi
 d. 2 dips

The answers are in the back of the book. If you don't know the answers, you can sneak a peak, but if you want to really know what all this means, do your own research and you will remember it like a champ.

ANS KEY

CREATIVE SUBMISSION STRATEGY

I want you to get noticed. I want you to be different than those other guys and girls. I want you to rock! To accomplish all these things I want you to develop a "creative submission strategy." This is a strategy to get your resume in the hands of the right people and make an impact. The following section is about getting you noticed; getting your resume maximum play.

How can you send your resume to get noticed? Let's start simple. I knew a very successful publicist and her job was to get busy editors of glossy entertainment and fashion mags to concentrate on her clients for editorial coverage. She explained to me that one trick of the trade is to send your info or resume in an 8.5x11 clear plastic envelope. That way everyone knows that the mail isn't junk mail or a solicitation for 2-for-1 pizzas...mmm, pizza. There is also something hypnotic about this technique, makes the reader take notice and actually read the documents. You can use a simple cover letter over your resume to hide your personal details until it's opened.

The Never Ending Stories

I have told the same stories about ten thousand times and I still smile when I think about them. In my career I have always been the least skilled candidate for the job, but that has never, ever stopped me from chasing some great opportunities. What I lacked in skills or experience I made up in hustle. The following stories are examples of creative submissions and unabashed hustle.

Vertigo (Do not try this at home or anywhere else)

I am afraid of heights, but I am not afraid of making money. I had heard about this sweet sales gig in Los Angeles. Basically, it involved going to small fashion boutiques (existing accounts) and merchandising this accessories line and taking reorders. It would pay me around 100,000 plus a car allowance and take about 40 hours a week. Hey, no cold calling, just pretty up their stores and take fill-in orders? I was up for that. I knew somebody that knew somebody that had a cousin that worked for these guys. The tip I got was that when I sent my resume, I was supposed to send my resume in a creative way.

What does that mean? I don't consider myself a creative dude. I initially had visions of handing my resume to the sales manager at his house. That seemed a bit stalker-ish. I thought about skywriting a message over their corporate office instructing them to read my resume. I realized that was too expensive and risky...what if no one looked up? I even considered sending it as a singing telegram. I thought that might be funny and scary. Funny equals good, scary equals bad. I met my inside source for lunch later that week and we were sitting on a popular street at one of those outdoor sidewalk cafes. I looked up and saw a billboard for his company. It was about thirty feet high and I am very scared of heights. I summoned the courage and had my companion snap a picture of me nervously pressed against the billboard. In retrospect it was pretty dumb and probably illegal. I was sure I was going to pancake myself on Sunset Blvd. Alas, the picture turned out great. I blew it up to 8.5 x 11 and used it as my cover sheet. I sent my resume and jazzy cover sheet to the sales manager. And, I got the job. The sales manager said if I was willing to scale that billboard then he could only imagine what I would do for him in the field.

Giant Cookie

I was working at a major surfwear chain and I didn't quite fit in. They wanted me in Quiksilver Flannels not Nicole Miller Ties (which were rad at the time). I really did like working for this company and I was a decent manager, but after being passed over for a key promotion my eye started to wander. My favorite shopping spot was the newly opened Macy's Men's Store at South Coast Plaza in Costa Mesa, CA. That Macy's credit card was always maxed. Calvin Klein started making bridge-priced dress shirts and ties and I loved them. I wondered how cool it would be to be a sales rep for Calvin Klein. I was sure I could do the job even though I had zero experience in wholesale sales. I was obsessed with making it happen.

> I was working at a major surfwear chain and I didn't quite fit in. They wanted me in Quiksilver Flannels not Nicole Miller Ties

A plan was formulated, in retrospect, the plan was a bit aggressive and stalker-ish, but nevertheless it was a plan. I was going to:

A) Find the number to Calvin Klein HQ in NYC
B) Find out who the VP of Sales was
C) Make contact with the VP of Sales
D) Convince him to hire me to rep the west coast and pay me a load of money!

Steps A and B were within my range, C seemed a bit out of my control and D was ridiculous, but I didn't care. What did I have to lose; I still had my job and I was young, bold and slightly obnoxious. Nothing was going to change those facts. So, I found the number to Calvin Klein HQ in NYC.

I called and asked to speak with the Vice President of Sales. "Which one", the receptionist asked. Click, I hung up. I wasn't prepared for that question. I panicked and regrouped. Again, the receptionist answered and I asked to speak to the Vice President of Shirts and Ties. She said, "You mean the Vice President of Sales for Dress Furnishings?" I said, "Yes." She asked me what company I was with. I hung up. Oh, I was not expecting that one. This lady was tough. I thought I'd better wait a day or two and try again. I knew I had to ask for the VP of Sales for Dress Furnishings and I had to be from a company.

I called back two days later and asked to speak with the VP of Dress Furnishings and I told the receptionist it was, "Adam Reiter from Adam's Stores." Yes, that was the best I could come up with. She asked me to hold. Finally, I was being transferred to the VP of Shirts and Ties. I was so nervous. The receptionist came back on and said he was in a meeting and that I could leave my name, number and reason why I was calling and she would forward the message. I left my name, my pager number and told her I was interested in the shirts and ties and to tell him I loved the product. She promised to relay the message. I thought that was an awesome message, sure to light up my pager with "Mr. Shirts and Ties" digits. After two weeks of frantically checking every page, no calls were received from CK HQ. Most people would have probably left it at that and moved on, but I was dumb and I had this amazing drive to meet this person.

Persistence and Pennies

I kept calling and getting the same deal from the receptionist, "I'll pass on the message." I didn't know this person's name so it was hard for me to get by her. I needed a new plan. I knew a guy whose dad was the CEO of a big parts company. He said half of the calls his secretary got were complaints that customers wanted to address with him because they wanted action. His say was the bottom line for his company and customers knew that. I asked him if he took all the calls and he said he took some each day, but mostly his secretary handled all of the calls and transferred customers to the correct departments for resolution.

Hmmm, my little brain started cranking out a plan. The next day I called CK again, but instead of asking for "Mr. Shirts and Ties" I demanded to speak to the CEO. The receptionist asked why and I just kept insisting to speak with the CEO. She transferred me to his assistant. When the assistant answered I apologized and said I was actually trying to reach the VP of Sales for Dress Furnishings. She said, "Oh, Joe Klein, yes, let me transfer you." When the call came from the CEO's office, guess who picked up? Joe Klein, "Mr. Shirts and Ties!" I think I swallowed my tongue because all I could muster was a loud wheezing sound. He kept saying, "Hello, hello." Then, like a quarter horse busting through the starting gate I blurted, "Hi, it's so nice to finally speak with you. I love your product and I just have to meet you and I know when you meet me you'll know what a dedicated and hard working asset I could be for you…"

He asked me to breathe. He asked me my name; I left that part out. Then, he asked me if this was a joke. I gathered myself and explained my passion for his products and my desire to move from retail to wholesale sales. He was trying to get me off the phone and direct me to HR, but I kept telling him about the product I had seen in stores and opportunities he was missing in my market. He was gracious and spent another ten minutes on the phone with me. He explained he already had a sales staff and that because this is a new product launch he had to hire sales professionals that have the relationships with buyers of major accounts. I told him I understood and I thanked him for his time. Again, this would have been the end of this story for most.

Getting to D

I had accomplished A, B and C and all I had left was D. Another plan began to boil. I decided to go to all of the major accounts that I knew carried the CK product in my area and ask managers from these stores about the product and how the other product sells. They thought I was a super well-informed shopper and gave me their opinion on colors, prints and fabrications. Some even shared information on fit issues and product placement issues on their retail floor. I wrote notes on every visit and compiled them in a report. On my lunch break one day, I went to the cookie place in the food court and had them make me a special treat.

> "Are you crazy, I don't know if I should be scared of you or hire you?"

A few days later I got a page from NYC. It was Mr. Shirts and Ties! I called him and this time the receptionist put me right through. "Are you crazy, I don't know if I should be scared of you or hire you?" He received my treat, a 24 inch cookie with "meet me" spelled in frosting. I also sent my notes from my shopping recon. I said I was coming to NYC and I would love to just buy him lunch or coffee or something. He agreed to have lunch with me. I saved my pennies to get a ticket out there, had a place to crash and off I went. We went for a Manhattan lunch and Joe told me about the business, how he got into it and a bit about his wife and kids. I hung on every word. The bill came and this Manhattan lunch broke my bank. I paid and we went our separate ways. I spent so much money on lunch I didn't quite have enough for a return ticket (In the back of my mind I believed he was going to offer me a job right there in NYC). Mommy! My mom sent me the return ticket.

Over the next six months I called Joe, asked about his family and inquired about the business. He would sometimes send me shirts and line sheets. I would give my feedback. Our conversations were always short, but he always took my calls and that felt like a success to me. I had decided to try to change gears and look for other jobs.

I was just getting calls back for interviews for mediocre jobs when Joe called. "I got a ticket for you, I need you on a plane for NYC on Thursday. Can you do it?" Ummm, hello! Yes! "I just had a guy quit and I need another West Coast Rep." "I am going to have you train out here and then we'll set you up in LA." The call ended. My body was numb. I didn't understand what just happened. What happened was that I got the gig I had chased for almost a year, I was doing something new and exciting and finally making some real money. I got to D!

Hustle

When I decide I want something I sometimes think about the reasons why I can't get what I want. Then, I remind myself that this is my lifetime, my shot and my moment to succeed. Sure, I have failed loads of times, but what I remember the best are the times I succeeded. The common thread in all of my wins wasn't my Brad Pitt looks, J Lo dance moves or my Einstein smarts. It was my desire to get what I want and the hustle I mustered to get there.

What Nobody Does

I think of resumes as walls. They are often the walls candidates can hide behind instead of really putting themselves out there. Don't get me wrong, you need a good resume, but you also need to make a good impression. What's to stop you from reaching out to the head buyer at your favorite store and introducing yourself as someone trying to break into the business? What's to stop you from calling the VP of Design for your favorite brand and telling her you are a fashion design student trying to get more insight into the business and asking her if it would be possible to buy her a cup of coffee?

> Don't get me wrong, you need a good resume, but you also need to make a good impression.

The people that you want to directly work for are in the grind of their daily routines. You don't think they would love to hear from someone who loves and appreciates what they do and wants to buy them lunch or a cup of coffee? Come on, everyone loves that kind of flattery and every boss is always on the look out for raw talent, somebody that does something different. If you put yourself out there and stick with it, you will be surprised to see how many people will meet you more than half way.

Submitting Your Resume Online

It's totally fine to send your resumes to an e-mail address of a job you saw online. That's the way most do it these days. However, you are not part of the "most" crowd. You are the next great fashion designer, buyer, PR pro, etc. So, why not really show them what you've got and start meeting some cool people?

Now, what do you do when people want to meet you? Let's move on to the next step...the Interview.

YOU CAN
GET A JOB
in
FASHION!

THE INTERVIEW

I have been on my share of unsuccessful dates–plenty. When I complained to my father about the recurring nightmares where I kept drowning in the dating pool, he offered me one piece of super sage advice. "Be quiet and listen; get your dates to talk about themselves and let me know how that works." So, instead of telling my dates how cool I was, I was supposed to ask them questions and get them to really talk about themselves and, at least, pretend to be more than interested. My dad's gold nuggets of advice turned into the best dates ever! I became so good at asking and listening, getting people to talk about themselves, that I started using this technique without realizing it. Suddenly, personal and professional opportunities popped up all over the place. Hey, people like talking about themselves and for some weird reason they love the people who are a willing audience when they are talking about themselves. Weird. And awesome!

Indeed, the best interviews of my life happened using this technique. I would conduct research about the company beforehand, a lot of research (using the tools I have shown you) and when given the opportunity I would start asking questions. You know the end of an interview where you are asked if, "You have any questions?" Well, I had a lot of questions for the interviewer about how they liked working for the company and what they loved about their job and any piece of interest I had picked up by listening throughout the interview. The interviewer was left thinking I was interested in the company, passionate about my career and had a lot of positive energy. "I think you would be a good fit for our company," was a line I got a lot after interviews. After all, every hiring manager is looking for skills and personality. They want potential employees to get their company vibe.

> The interviewer was left thinking that I was interested in the company, passionate about my career and had a lot of positive energy

The Anatomy of an Interview

Anyone for a little baseball? The interview is like pitching a complete game. There are three parts to an Interview:

The Warm Up (Getting to Know You)
The Game (Your Skills)
The Ninth Inning (Sealing The Deal)

The Warm Up

I have stressed how important personality is and the beginning of your interview is the time to set the tone. This is the part of the interview where you give off your vibe, get to know the interviewer and plan your strategy. Your vibe is conveyed through your appearance, your walk and your talk. Dressing correctly for an interview is so important in the fashion industry. You should dress in line with the company aesthetic. Now, if this is an action sports company, a lingerie manufacturer or a kid's clothier you're going to have to use your best judgment. Don't show up to a lingerie interview in booty shorts, please! I always tell people to err on the side of more formal than less formal. But, the bottom line is you have to look like you understand fashion and the company look. A company's website is the best starting point to discover their vibe. You can usually find their current look books/catalogs on their site.

My wife always wears an item she has made to an interview. More often than not, a hiring manager will ask where she got her top and she will tell them she made it. That little deal usually puts her a long way towards sealing the deal. Pay extra close attention to your interviewer. They will subconsciously be giving you clues about the company, the job and how to land the job. When an interviewer repeats themselves it is a subconscious "self-reminder" to emphasize qualities they are looking for in the successful candidate. Make mental note of these oral cues and make sure to emphasize your skills as they pertain to the clues the interviewer gives you. The most important thing to remember during the *Warm Up* is to try to create a connection with the interviewer. And how do you do that? Ask questions and listen. Remember, it's a date!

> *To interview is like going on a blind date, you have a short period of time to get to know each other and decide if there will be a second date. During the interview it is just as important for the candidate to get to know you, the position and company as it is for you to assess the candidate's skill set and if a good chemistry exists between the candidate and company.*
>
> **Merle Sloss**
> **EVP/President of Licensing**
> **Geoffrey Beene**

The Game

Every good pitcher in baseball relies on more than just a flame thrower arm or a wicked knuckle ball. They study their opponents. They know what kind of pitches a hitter likes and they devise a plan to pitch to the hitters weaknesses. Part of your interview preparation is doing research on the company, knowing who the players are and news about the company. You should be well versed in this area, by now.

The most important part of your game time preparation is to study the job description for the gig you are applying for. Take each part of the job description and job qualifications and write them down on flash cards. Write on the flip side of the cards an example of how you excelled at each one of the qualifications and requirements. During the interview, the hiring manager will likely go through a routine. You need to steer the interview back to your base of knowledge and skills. You have to try to impress the hiring manager with the knowledge you garnered through your company research. That should rock them from their routine and really shift the attention and interest to you in a very positive way.

The Ninth Inning

Have you ever seen the movie Ground Hog Day? Bill Murray, the lead actor, goes to sleep every night and wakes up to the same day over and over and over again. When I watch the movie I am always waiting for Bill's character, Phil, to do something different so he can just get through to tomorrow. I have been through my own bout of Ground Hog Day. Geez, how many interviews did I blow? Too many! Man, the interviews usually went great, I said the right things, I made a connection with the interviewer and then nothing. After so many failed interviews I had to go through each interview to figure out what I was doing wrong. I always felt uneasy at the end of an interview. I never knew how to end an interview. Inevitably, the interview would wind down, the interviewer would ask me if I had any other questions, I would say no and leave. I did all the work, the research, the schmoozing and then... Why didn't I just close the interview? I started asking more questions when asked if I had any more questions. "What kind of bagels should I bring tomorrow?" The hiring manager laughed, relaxed and said, "Well, I like egg bagels, but let me talk to the department head and see when we can get you in here." Bang, a strike! My close was aggressive, but kind of funny. I developed a whole bunch of closes designed to give me some hint of where I stood. I could give you my lines, but I want you to develop your own. They must sound natural so make sure they are closing lines you would naturally say.

> Once I added this final piece to my game, my success rate in interviews skyrocketed. It will for you, too...

Once I added this final piece to my game, my success rate in interviews skyrocketed. It will for you, too, if you concentrate on each part of your game. After a few interviews you will be a big league pitcher, promise.

And Practice

Your teachers and colleagues are great to use for practice interviewing. The number one issue faced by most people I coach is over-thinking an interview. If you have your research in your head and feel comfortable with your skills then you should have no problem. Practice with job descriptions you like and have your teachers or colleagues quiz you about qualifications listed in the job descriptions. Give them your research notes and have them quiz you about the companies in your research. Try to answer a question and then ask your interviewer a question about their job or their company to get them to talk about themselves. Once you get comfortable talking about your successes and getting the hiring managers to talk about themselves, you will ace your interviews.

conclusion:
MY FINAL THOUGHTS

Here comes the wind-beneath-your-wings speech. You can get the job you want, no problem. I know you can get it because I know what it takes. And here's the kicker...***now you know too***. If you have read this far and done the tasks and exercises I have asked you to do, you are doing more than 99% of the other people trying to get the many great gigs in this biz. But seriously, most candidates who see a job they like just know they are going to get it and if they don't they lose interest. That is, if they know what they really want to do in this business to begin with. But that's not you. You know what you want do.

The good news is, if you have executed all the steps in this book, then you have picked a career direction, built a winning resume, learned how to research, formulated a creative submission strategy and are well on your way to landing some interviews and that sweet job in fashion. Nothing is standing your way. Go get it.

If you've already sealed the deal on your sweet fashion job, you rock! If you haven't gotten a great job yet, you will. Just hustle, be persistent and you will get a great job.

I have packed the back of the book with some useful terms, cool websites and a load of job descriptions. Use this book as a reference guide now and throughout your career. It doesn't matter if you are a student or a seasoned veteran, everyone needs a refresher from time to time.

> I am confident that you will have some great wins to share and I want to hear them

Also, I want to hear from you. Tell me about your job search, your hurdles and successes. I am confident you will have some great wins to share and I want to hear them so I can gloat to my mom when she asks me again why I never became a lawyer.

RESOURCES & WORKSHEETS

Definitions, salary ranges, resumes, worksheets, templates, sites and more!

Careers

Below is a compilation of jobs in fashion (retail and wholesale). I have included salary ranges and some notes. Look for the **SBJ** designation for Adam's Secret Backdoor Jobs.

Fashion Design and Production Jobs

Accessories Designer (SBJ)- Concept, design and develop fashion accessories. I like niche design jobs because most people who go into fashion want to be a women's or men's designer. There aren't as many accessory design jobs, but there also aren't as many accessory designers.
Salary Ranges:
Entry-$25,000-35,000
Mid-level-$40,000-80,000
Senior/Executive-$100,000-225,000

Apparel Designer- Concept, design and develop fashion apparel. This is the job I am most asked about and competition is fierce. But, advancement can be lightning fast and opportunities exist all over the country.
Salary Ranges:
Entry-$25,000-35,000
Mid-level-$40,000-80,000
Senior/Executive-$100,000-1,200,000

Costing-Designate the cost of manufactured goods. This is a finance job. Titles for this job might be Costing Analyst, Manager of Costing and Costing Director. More often these roles are being included in other finance jobs, but these jobs do exist.
Salary Ranges:
Entry-$32,000-45,000
Mid-level-$40,000-80,000
Senior/Executive-$80,000-120,000

Cutter-Precision cuts fabric/patterns. This is an entry-point job that can lead to other jobs like marker making and patternmaking.
Salary Range:
All Levels-$18,000-40,000

Footwear Designer- Concept, design and develop footwear. If I could have been any kind of designer in this business I would have been a footwear designer. It is a very technical craft and there is always a need for both fashion and athletic footwear designers.
Salary Ranges:
Entry-$25,000-35,000
Mid-level-$40,000-80,000
Senior/Executive-$100,000-225,000

Forecasting/Trend-Predict and track fashion trends in design, fabrication, color and vibe. This was the IT job to have ten years ago. Due to budget cuts and the proliferation of fashion forecasting services and online resources these jobs have dwindled. They still exist, but generally only at large companies.

Salary Ranges:
Entry-$25,000-45,000
Mid-level-$40,000-80,000
Senior/Executive-$80,000-150,000

Fit Model (**SBJ**)-Model designs for design/ production teams to determine fit quality. Most of these gigs are contract/part-time hourly positions. But, it is a great way to meet designers and production staff and that is why I designated it an **SBJ** job.

Salary Ranges:
All Levels: $15hr.-150/hr.

Grader-Adjusts pattern size for spectrum of apparel sizes. This is another job that is tied to pattern making and can lead to a pattern making job.

Salary Ranges:
All Levels:$18,000-40,000

Intimates Designer (SBJ)-Concept, design and develop underwear, hosiery, loungewear and lingerie. Another great design niche with a smaller field of competition. I believe this is a growing segment of design.

Salary Ranges:
Entry-$25,000-45,000
Mid-level-$40,000-80,000
Senior/Executive-$80,000-150,000

Marker Maker-Marks fabric for pattern cutting. This is another job that can lead to a pattern making job.

Salary Ranges:
All Levels:$18,000-40,000

Merchandiser (**SBJ**)-Manages the business side of design, tracking historical data (sales, sell-through), managing target costs and configuring assortments. Some joke that merchandisers are frustrated designers, but more often than not designers have to execute both roles, designer and merchandiser. There are still loads of merchandising jobs out there.

Salary Ranges:
Entry-$35,000-45,000
Mid-level-$65,000-120,000
Senior/Executive-$120,000-500,000

Patternmaker (**SBJ**)-Creates patterns used to produce apparel. A great patternmaker is the gold standard for design companies. Openings for awesome pattern makers are abundant.

Salary Ranges:
Entry-$18,000-45,000
Mid-level-$45,000-75,000
Senior/Executive-$80,000-125,000

Piece Goods/Trim Buyer-Sources and purchases fabric and trims for production. I am always fascinated to hear about how people get into this job because I never hear people say, "I want to become a Trim Buyer when I grow up." Nevertheless, this is a great job.

Salary Ranges:
Entry-$30,000-45,000
Mid-level-$45,000-75,000
Senior/Executive-$80,000-100,000

Product Developer (**SBJ**)-Manages product development process from concept to delivery. This job takes responsibility once design hands off their designs for sampling and stays on top of the product until it hits stores. These jobs have been popping up all over the place.

Salary Ranges:
Entry-$30,000-45,000
Mid-level-$45,000-75,000
Senior/Executive-$80,000-120,000

Product/Brand Manager (SBJ)-Oversees design, marketing and sales of product. This gig is often tied to marketing and incorporates management of sales, design production and sometimes finance. As more and more fashion companies become more corporate, more like other traditional consumer goods companies these jobs will become even more prevalent.
Salary Ranges:
Entry-$45,000-65,000
Mid-level-$65,000-100,000
Senior/Executive-$90,000-150,000

Production-Manages production processes of designed goods. There are two sides of production, pre-production and production. Production people with good domestic and overseas manufacturing connections are always in demand.
Salary Ranges:
Entry-$18,000-45,000
Mid-level-$50,000-100,00
Senior/Executive-$90,000-150,000

Quality Control-Inspects and ensures desired quality of garments being produced. This job requires a lot of local and/or international travel to manufacturers.
Salary Ranges:
Entry-$18,000-35,000
Mid-level-$40,000-70,000
Senior/Executive-$70,000-100,000

Sales-Sell goods to retailers for a company or for multiple companies. There are corporate sales reps (inside and outside), Independent sales reps and multi-line showroom reps that represent multiple lines out of one showroom. Companies always need great sales people with great relationships with retailers.
Salary Ranges:
Entry-$25,000-35,000
Mid-level-$40,000-100,000
Senior/Executive-$100,000-500,000

Samplemaker-Creates samples based on designs. Finding good samplemakers is tough, too. Great samplemakers are always in high demand.
Salary Ranges:
All Levels:$18,000-50,000

Sewer-Sew fabric and trims into garments. Good sewers can always find jobs in fashion.
Salary Ranges:
All Levels:$16,000-40,000

Stylist-Puts together looks and the overall feel for photoshoots with fashion designers and media editors. It can also be a reference to someone that is a personal shopper and someone that puts together looks for high profile people.
Salary Ranges:
All Levels:$18,000-500,000

Technical Designer (SBJ)-Creates the blueprints for designs to be used in production. Pay for technical designers maintain a steady increase from year to year. Advancement for technical designers is swift.
Salary Ranges:
Entry-$35,000-55,000
Mid-level-$60,000-100,000
Senior/Executive-$100,000-175,000

Retail Jobs
(I left out all of the store, field and related retail operations positions to concentrate on the more fashion positions in retail)

Allocator (SBJ)-Partners with Buyers and Planners to analyze sales and allocate merchandise to stores. A job that very few people go to school for has an easier entry-point than buying jobs and may spring board to a buying or planning job.
Salary Ranges:
Entry-$35,000-55,000
Mid-level-$60,000-100,000
Senior/Executive-$100,000-125,000

Buyer-Buys products to sell through retail channels. I have seen a slow decline in buying jobs, but mostly at the associate level. There are still plenty of buying jobs for people with a great product sense and a shrewd business mind.
Salary Ranges:
Entry-$28,000-55,000
Mid-level-$60,000-100,000
Senior/Executive-$100,000-500,000

Fashion Director-Directs trends for buying office and might also direct the store look at the retail level. These jobs are just awesome, but like fashion forecasting jobs, are not in abundance. These jobs are usually given to people promoted from the buying office.
Salary Ranges:
All Levels-$80,000-$180,000

Merchandise/Retail Coordinator-Ensures proper look and placement of product at retailers. This position acts as a separate set of eyes for a brand sales and marketing teams to see what is happening at retail accounts.
Salary Ranges:
Entry-$18,000-35,000
Mid-level-$35,000-65,000
Senior/Executive-$70,000-150,000

Planner (SBJ)-Uses historical data to determine what product goes into what stores. Planners are always in demand and great planners are hard to find. Planners can have a very fast promotion track.
Salary Ranges:
Entry-$35,000-55,000
Mid-level-$60,000-100,000
Senior/Executive-$100,000-185,000

Store Designer-Concept, design and develop new stores. This job requires a degree in architecture and awesome CAD and graphic skills. I threw this one in because there is a push to develop enticing, brand building retail environments and I love it!
Salary Ranges:
Entry-$55,000-75,000
Mid-level-$75,000-125,000
Senior/Executive-$125,000-200,000

Visual Merchandiser-Styles the appearance of merchandise displays in stores. A lot of people like this job. To get a flavor of what these people do, go to your favorite ritzy shopping area and gaze at the windows of Neimans, Saks and Ralph Lauren.
Salary Ranges:
Entry-$25,000-45,000
Mid-level-$45,000-75,000
Senior/Executive-75,000-225,000

Other Fashion Jobs
Fashion Editor-Manages fashion content for TV, publications or other media. These jobs are great once you get there, but you certainly need to pay your dues to get there.
Salary Ranges:
Entry-$25,000-45,000
Mid-level-$45,000-75,000
Senior/Executive-75,000-150,000

Graphic Designer-Creates graphics for print, web or products. Graphic jobs can lead to Art Director jobs and Creative Director jobs (also a marketing job). There is no shortage of graphic jobs available.
Salary Ranges:
Entry-$25,000-45,000
Mid-level-$45,000-75,000
Senior/Executive-75,000-350,000

Marketing-Concept, develop and execute marketing strategies. Marketing has become so exciting and diverse now that most companies leverage the reach of the net to send their messages. It's an exciting time to be in marketing.
Salary Ranges:
Entry-$25,000-45,000
Mid-level-$45,000-75,000
Senior/Executive-75,000-350,000

Public Relations-Manage communications to the community, your market and the media. A quick note on publicists, this my friends, is a job for the ultimate networker.
Salary Ranges:
Entry-$18,000-45,000
Mid-level-$45,000-75,000
Senior/Executive-75,000-200,000

Blank Resume Template

NAME
_____

Address   Phone Number   e-mail Address

Objective Statement: (Enter statement here. Need help getting started? Go back to page 27 for tips on writing an effective objective statement)

Work Experience:

(**Company Name of Most Recent Job**)   (Employment Dates)
(Job Title)
- First accomplishment
- Second accomplishment
- Third accomplishment
- Fourth accomplishment
- Fifth accomplishment

(**Name of Most Recent Job**)   (Employment Dates)
(Job Title)
- First accomplishment
- Second accomplishment
- Third accomplishment
- Fourth accomplishment
- Fifth accomplishment

(**Name of Most Recent Job**)   (Employment Dates)
(Job Title)
- First accomplishment
- Second accomplishment
- Third accomplishment
- Fourth accomplishment
- Fifth accomplishment

Education: (Enter Name of College and Location)
(Enter degree or degree you are pursuing)

Skills: (Enter your relevant skills here)

References available upon request

TERESA A. WILLIS

600 East Fun Street
Columbus, OH 43202
Phone: 216-555-5555
e-mail: willis22@gmail.com

OBJECTIVE:
To obtain a position where I can leverage my technical design skills to enhance a creative team in the contemporary sportswear market.

EXPERIENCE:

Express Columbus, OH
Technical Design Coordinator: Men's Knits and Wovens   1/2007-Present
- Sole development liaison for $50 million program produced in factories in Hong Kong, Indonesia and India.
- Developed technical spec manual and fit communications manual to aid in expediting the approval process and staying on calendar.
- Train new assistant designers in Web PDM and handoff procedures.
- Spearheaded team to confirm label accuracies and standards.
- Created store audit logs for review of product fit and quality standards for product that has hit the sales floor.

Lane Bryant Columbus, OH   8/2006-1/2007
Product Development Intern: Casual Knit Tops
- Produced style reports for over 200 sku's per season.
- Created new concept presentations for all meetings in product development.
- Developed and initiated the Web PDM process, completing all product development portions, for all styles to be sampled, with emphasis on PDM sketches.
- Reclassified and updated fabric library to reflect new product classifications.

Ann Taylor Columbus, OH   1/2005-8/2006
Assistant Sales Manager
- Recruited area sales associates from Banana Republic, Club Monaco and other competitors.
- Increased 2006 sales by 36% over same stores sales from last year.
- Decreased shrink by 26% representing a $26,000 savings for this $2,000,000 store.

EDUCATION:
The Ohio State University, Columbus, OH
Bachelor's of Science degree Fashion Merchandising and Product Development

SKILLS:
Microsoft Office Suite 2007, CAD (Micro Graphics Designer, Lectra Kaleido, Adobe Photoshop, Illustrator, Designer, Painter, Easy Coloring, Easy Weave).

References available upon request

ADAM FORTUNAS

50 Bigtimes Ave., Apt 104 Boston, MA 02215
Hm (781) 699-5555
Adamfortu@yahoo.com

PROFESSIONAL
EXPERIENCE:

Filenes/Kaufmann's, Division of Federated, Boston, MA   Oct. 2005-Present
Assistant Buyer, Women's Fashion Jewelry

- Executed all store orders for $40 million business in 97 doors.
- Developed margin analysis system to accurately pick markdown opportunities.
- Managed Open to Buy for $10 million worth of business.
- Created advertising layout for weekly direct mail and circular books.
- Sourced new vendor opportunities resulting in the introduction of Judith Jack Jewelry, the number one trending resource for 2007, representing a 72% sell-through.

Saks Fifth Avenue, NYC, NY   Sept. 2004-Oct. 2005
Allocation Analyst, Men's Dress Furnishings

- Allocated all sportswear for a $60 million dollar business in 180 doors.
- Analyzed vendor size and width selling to identify new opportunities resulting in a standard for vendor evaluation.
- Proactive management of product shipping/logistics from factory to warehouse yielded a $2 million savings from late shipping vendors.

Saks Fifth Avenue, NYC, NY   Aug. 2004-Oct. 2005
Planning Intern, Men's Accessories

- Managed planning responsibilities for accessories for a 5-door $5 million dollar business.
- Developed and created accessory assortments for each of the unique concept stores.

EDUCATION:
Rollins College, Winter Park, FL
Bachelor of Arts in Economics

SKILLS:
SAP, Arthur Allocation, JDA, AS400, Windows, Lotus Notes, Microsoft Word, Excel, Fluent in Spanish, Conversational in Mandarin.

References available upon request

Kara Morse

146 West Happy Street, NY, NY 10012 (212) 554- 5555 Karamorse@gmail.com
Online Design Portfolio: www.karamorsedesigns.com

Career Goal: To obtain a design position in the fashion industry where I can utilize my design and merchandising skills to contribute to a growing creative team.

Work Experience:

American Apparel, New York, New York   April 2008-Present
Design Intern

- Sourced overseas markets in India and Japan for new fabric and trim concepts.
- Sketched 33 bodies for upcoming men's and women's collections.
- Designed color cards, swatch books and concept boards.
- Researched competitors products and target markets.
- Developed salesman's line sheets and look books for upcoming season.

Armani Exchange, New York, NY   December 2007- Present
Sales Associate

- Designed Spring windows for new David Beckham campaign launch.
- Awarded Sales Award for largest increase over personal plan for January in the region.
- Produced A/X fashion show for American Cancer Society fundraiser.
- Communicate monthly with buying office on "best sellers" to improve merchandise mix for store.

Education: Katharine Gibbs School, New York, New York
Currently pursuing A.A.S Fashion Design and Merchandising
Graduating June, 2009

Skills: Microsoft Excel and Word, PowerPoint, Photoshop, and Illustrator.

References available upon request

ADAM FORTUNAS

50 Bigtimes Ave., Apt 104 Boston, MA 02215
Hm (781) 699-5555
Adamfortu@yahoo.com

Dream Society Fashion
Attn: Julie Hertz, Director of Human Resources
1222 Dream Street, Suite 430
Dream City, NY 10001

September 12, 2008

Dear Ms. Hertz,

I am submitting my resume for your consideration in response to your ad in the May 5th edition of the NY Times for a Design Director. Working for stalwart contemporary brands like Theory and Donna Karan as a Design Director has afforded me the ability to develop myself as a creative manager. Beyond recruiting, team development and concept building, I have helped Theory launch two new product lines resulting in a $30,000,000 business over the last two years. I read an article in WWD that suggested the Dream Society was looking into branching out into Boys and Outerwear and those two categories are the categories I launched for Theory. I have followed the success of Dream Society for the past five years. I am really excited about the brand's growth and look forward to meeting with you to tell you more about my history and discuss what I can do to help foster continued growth for your remarkable brand.

Warmest Regards,

Adam Fortunas
(954) 322-3456 (cell)

The Research Worksheet

Use the provided worksheet templates to conduct your Fashion A-List, B-List and C-List exercises. Placing the book on a photocopier or carefully removing the template page to do so, make 20 copies. Label and number the sheets as seen below as you fill in the research criteria detailed on page 36. Remember you need 10 A-List companies, 50 B-List companies and 40 C-List companies to complete the exercise. You'll find a Retail Research sheet on the next page. So get jammin' and you'll be on your way to finding your ideal fashion job.

Fashion **A**-List Research Worksheet			#s **1** - **5**
Company	**Facts & Figures**	**Management**	**Senses**
Abc Knits www.abcco.com 123 A Street Salinas, CA 93333 831-422-2222	$23 Million Jr.s Design Co. Just launched 1st US Store Signed Kmart Licensing Deal	Jan Berger VP, Design Mike Simms Design Director (was with Wet Seal)	Jr.s knit tops, denim and sweaters. See online at Delias.com

Fashion ____-List Research Worksheet   #s ____-____

Company	Facts & Figures	Management	Senses

Retail ___-List Research Worksheet

#s _____-_____

Company	Facts & Figures	Management	Senses

Quiz Answers:

Retail MS Office Quiz

1)d
2)b
3)a
4)a
5)d
6)d
7)a
8)d
9)d
10)c

Fashion Illustrator Quiz

1)b
2)a
3)c
4)b
5)a
6)d
7)b

Research Resource Sites:

In no way do I endorse these sites, they are just some sites I have visited
that you might enjoy and may also help you in your research

Blogs:
purseblog.com
shoewawa.com
shoeblogs.com
baglady.tv
iamfashion.blogspot.com
thebudgetfashionista.com
catwalkqueen.tv
stylebakery.com
denimology.co.uk
shefinds.com/blog
thesartorialist.blogspot.com
bagsnob.com
stylecritics.com
myfashionlife.com
highsnobiety.com
fashion-incubator.com/mt
hypebeast.com
fashionologie.com
therunwayscoop.com
nitrolicious.com/blog
freshnessmag.com
shopaholicsdaily.com
stylebubble.typepad.com
facehunter.blogspot.com
coquette.blogs.com
bergdorfgoodman.blogpost.com

Fashion News Sites:
hintmag.com
fashiontribes.typepad.com
WWD.com
lookonline.com
dnrnews.com
apparelnews.net
just-style.com
dailycandy.com
fashionwiredaily.com
footwearnews.com
chainstoreage.com
cottoninc.com
retailingtoday.com
licensemag.com
lucire.com
luxuryfashion.com
sportswearnet.com
style.com
nrf.com

Job Sites:
allretailjobs.com
kristopherdukes.com
omiru.com
sassybella.com
frugal-fashionista.blogspot.com
secondcitystyle.blogspot.com
whowhatweardaily.com
jcreport.com
stylecareers.com
fashioncareers.com
monster.com
hotjobs.com
careerbuilder.com
thefashiontool.com
theretailtool.com
fashionjobspro.com

Other Resource Sites:
hoovers.com
LAtimes.com
WSJ.com
cfda.com
calfashion.org

Bibliography:

TheJobTool.com 2007 salary survey

The bureau of laborstatistics.com

http://www.retailowner.com/Resources/GMROI/tabid/60/Default.aspx

http://office.microsoft.com/en-us/help/FX100485331033.aspx

http://www.reviseict.co.uk/lessons/powerpoint/assessmenttest.htm

http://www.chaminade.org/MIS/Tutorials/Quizzes/BasicWordQuiz1.htm

Sue Chastain, Graphics Software

http://graphicssoft.about.com/mbiopage.htm

The Job Tool © 2008
ISBN 978-0-615-26119-5